D0049593

The
BIG
BOOK
OF
SMALL
STUFF

ALSO BY THE AUTHOR

Don't Sweat the Small Stuff . . . and it's all small stuff

Don't Sweat the Small Stuff for Teens

Don't Sweat the Small Stuff in Love
(WITH KRISTINE CARLSON)

Don't Sweat the Small Stuff at Work

Don't Sweat the Small Stuff with Your Family

Don't Sweat the Small Stuff about Money

Slowing Down to the Speed of Life
(WITH JOSEPH BAILEY)

Handbook for the Heart
(WITH BENJAMIN SHIELD)

Handbook for the Soul
(WITH BENJAMIN SHIELD)

Shortcut Through Therapy

You Can Feel Good Again

You Can Be Happy No Matter What

Richard Carlson, Ph.D.

The

BIG
BOOK
OF
SMALL
STUFF

100 of the Best Inspirations from
DON'T SWEAT THE SMALL STUFF

NEW YORK

ISBN: 1-4013-0299-8

Hyperion books are available for special promotions and premiums. For details contact Michael Rentas, Assistant Director, Inventory Operations, Hyperion, 77 West 66th Street, 12th floor, New York, New York 10023, or call 212-456-0133.

Design by Karen Minster

FIRST EDITION

10 9 8 7 6 5 4 3 2 1

I dedicate this book to my daughters,
Jazzy and Kenna,
who remind me every day
how important it is to remember
not to "sweat the small stuff."
I love you both so much.
Thank you for
being just the way you are.

CONTENTS

ACKNOWLEDGMENTS . . . . *xiii*
INTRODUCTION . . . . *xv*

FROM
DON'T SWEAT THE SMALL STUFF

1. Don't Sweat the Small Stuff 3

2. Make Peace with Imperfection 4

3. Be Aware of the Snowball Effect of Your Thinking 6

4. Remind Yourself That When You Die,
   Your "In Basket" Won't Be Empty 8

5. Do Something Nice for Someone Else—
   and Don't Tell *Anyone* About It 10

6. Let Others Have the Glory 11

7. Learn to Live in the Present Moment 13

8. Ask Yourself the Question,
   "Will This Matter a Year from Now?" 15

9. Allow Yourself to Be Bored 16

10. Once a Week, Write a Heartfelt Letter 18

11. Repeat to Yourself, "Life Isn't an Emergency" 20

12. Imagine the People in Your Life as Tiny Infants
and as One-Hundred-Year-Old Adults...................... 22

13. Become a Better Listener................................ 23

14. Choose Your Battles Wisely............................. 25

15. Praise and Blame Are All the Same..................... 27

16. See the Innocence....................................... 29

17. Resist the Urge to Criticize........................... 31

18. Search for the Grain of Truth in Other Opinions 33

19. Become a Less Aggressive Driver........................ 34

20. Turn Your Melodrama into a Mellow-Drama 36

21. Think of What You Have Instead of What You Want......... 38

22. Stop Blaming Others 40

23. Transform Your Relationship to Your Problems 42

24. If Someone Throws You the Ball,
You Don't Have to Catch It............................... 44

25. Mind Your Own Business 46

26. Live This Day as if It Were Your Last. It Might Be! 48

FROM
DON'T SWEAT THE SMALL STUFF AT WORK

27. Dare to Be Happy...................................... 53

28. Become Less Controlling............................... 56

29. Don't Dramatize the Deadlines......................... 60

30. Remember the Phrase,
"Being Dead Is Bad for Business"......................... 62

31. Don't Sweat the Demanding Boss........................ 65

32. Don't Take the 20/80 Rule Personally 68

33. Make Friends with Your Receptionist 71

34. Be Careful What You Ask For 74

35. Absorb the Speed Bumps of Your Day 77

36. Never, Ever Backstab 80

37. Lower Your Expectations 83

38. Stop Wishing You Were Somewhere Else 86

39. Give Up Your Fear of Speaking to Groups 89

40. Avoid the Tendency to Put a Cost on Personal Things 91

41. When You Solicit Advice, Consider Taking It 94

42. Make Allowances for Incompetence 96

43. Don't Get Stressed by the Predictable 100

44. Don't Live in an Imagined Future 104

45. Admit That It's Your Choice 107

46. Learn to Delegate 110

47. Take Your Next Vacation at Home 113

48. Put Your Mind in Neutral 116

49. Remember the Whole Story 119

50. Don't Live for Retirement 122

FROM
DON'T SWEAT THE SMALL STUFF WITH YOUR FAMILY

51. Set a Positive Emotional Climate 127

52. Give Yourself an Extra Ten Minutes 129

53. Listen to Her (and Him Too) 131

54. Don't Answer the Phone 134

55. Encourage Boredom in Your Children 136

56. Expect It to Spill 138

57. Allow "White Space" in Your Calendar 140

58. Stop Exchanging Horror Stories 143

59. Never, Ever, Take Your Spouse
    (or Significant Other) for Granted 146

60. Don't Be a Martyr 149

61. When Someone Asks How You Are,
    Don't Emphasize How Busy You Are 151

62. Don't Go to Bed Mad 154

63. Have Family Meetings 156

64. Keep Your "Thought Attacks" in Check 158

65. Stop Repeating the Same Mistakes 161

66. Recognize When Someone Doesn't
    Have an Eye for Something 163

67. Have a Favorite Family Charity 166

68. Remind Yourself Frequently What Your
    Children Really Want 168

69. Remember, It's the Little Things That
    Will Be Remembered Most 170

70. Surrender to the Fact That There's Always Something to Do 173

71. Treat Your Family Members as if This Were
    the Last Time You Were Going to See Them 176

FROM

DON'T SWEAT THE SMALL STUFF FOR WOMEN

BY KRISTINE CARLSON

72. Wish Wonder Woman Good-bye 181

73. Cut Your Friends Some Slack 185

74. Perhaps It's Not Personal 188

75. Let Go of Your "Perfect" Plans 190

76. Don't Be a Backseat Driver 193

77. Go Ahead and Vent (One Time),
But Get It Off Your Chest 195

78. Rise Above the Rut of Your Routine 197

79. Say "No, but Thanks for Asking"
(Without Feeling Guilty) 199

80. Be 99 Percent Gossip-Free 202

81. Treasure the Journey 204

FROM

DON'T SWEAT THE SMALL STUFF IN LOVE

WITH KRISTINE CARLSON

82. Mostly, Be Pals 209

83. Learn to Laugh at Yourself 212

84. Throw Away Your Scorecard 215

85. Avoid the Words, "I Love You, But" 218

86. Remember That Your Partner Can't Read Your Mind 221

87. Don't Fight Over Stupid Things 223

88. Stop Wishing She (or He) Were Different 226

89. Jump-Start Your Relationship 229

90. Don't Sweat the Occasional Criticism 231

91. Avoid Correcting Each Other 234

92. Don't Let Your Children Come Between You 237

93. Say the Words, "I'm Sorry" 240

94. Treasure Each Other 243

FROM
DON'T SWEAT THE SMALL STUFF FOR MEN

95. Have an Affair 249

96. Don't Let the "Turkeys" Get You Down 252

97. Anticipate the Best 255

98. Consider That "Needing a Vacation"
    May Not Be the Real Problem 257

99. Let Others Be Right About the Little Things 259

100. Stop Broadcasting Your Thoughts 261

ACKNOWLEDGMENTS

I would like to acknowledge the following people for assisting me in the creation of this book: Patti Breitman for her enthusiasm and encouragement surrounding this book and for her dedication and wisdom in not sweating the small stuff. And Leslie Wells for her vision and for her insightful editorial skill.

Thank you both very much.

INTRODUCTION

It's hard to believe that ten years have passed since the original edition of *Don't Sweat the Small Stuff . . . and it's all small stuff* was written. Individually and collectively, our lives are very different from what they were back then. On an individual level, we have grown and matured. Those of us with children or grandchildren have seen them grow up before our eyes. Those without children have watched their friends and families do the same. On a collective level, life is vastly different than it once was. We now live in a post–9/11 world. Need I say more?

Then again, it seems, some things never change! We have the same capacity for joy that we have always had, and the same for laughter. And, unfortunately, we still have stress. Some of this stress, of course, is inevitable, just part of life—there's certainly nothing we can do about that.

Then there's all that everyday stuff to contend with—small stuff—that is around us twenty-four hours a day. We are lucky because there is something we can do about this: We can learn to not "sweat the small stuff."

Whether it's being stuck in a huge traffic jam, waiting "patiently" for a return phone call, watching someone talk with their mouth full, talking to someone who isn't listening, trying to find that lost set of keys, communicating with an officious bureaucrat, enduring unwarranted criticism, or the endless list of other possibilities, we can learn to transcend, and not be stressed by it. All it takes is a little practice, and, as importantly, knowing what to practice. We can learn, quite easily, that life is not the emergency we sometimes assume it to be!

That's where this book comes in handy. Over the past ten years, I have received a huge amount of feedback about which strategies for dealing with stress work best. It turns out that, although our external lives have changed a great deal during the past ten years, the most effective ways to live have not. We can learn to be less stressed, no matter what small stuff we face.

When our intention is to become more patient, forgiving, light-hearted, and better listeners, we can do that. When our wish is to slow down, smell the roses, cut ourselves and others more slack, we can do that, too. We can also become more loving, compassionate, humble, generous, philosophical, inwardly peaceful, and "present." All of this, and so much more, is simply a matter of perspective—and, of course, a little practice.

This is a book of one hundred of my favorite, as well as the most popular, strategies from the Don't Sweat series. I believe (and hope you will agree) that if you take these strategies to heart, your life will become less frustrating and more fun.

Life has always been, and will always be, a gift. In the absence of excess irritation and frustration, it's easier to experience it that way. As our stress is reduced, and as we feel less overwhelmed, the magic of life is renewed. We can see and experience the beauty that can often become invisible, or at least clouded, when we are bogged down with stress, or when little things are taking over our lives. As this happens, our relationships get better, our work becomes more interesting, and we are, most of the time, at peace.

It has been an honor and has brought me so much joy to hear from so many of you over the years. So whether you are a past reader of one or more of the Don't Sweat books, or a brand-new reader, my wish for you is exactly the same: I wish for you a life filled with love, happiness, and very little stress. I believe that there are two simple rules to make this happen: #1) Don't Sweat the Small Stuff, and #2) And it's all small stuff.

Treasure yourselves and the gift of life,
Richard Carlson

The
BIG
BOOK
OF
SMALL
STUFF

DON'T SWEAT THE SMALL STUFF
...and it's all small stuff

Don't Sweat the Small Stuff

Often we allow ourselves to get all worked up about things that, upon closer examination, *aren't* really that big a deal. We focus on little problems and concerns and blow them way out of proportion. A stranger, for example, might cut in front of us in traffic. Rather than let it go, and go on with our day, we convince ourselves that we are justified in our anger. We play out an imaginary confrontation in our mind. Many of us might even tell someone else about the incident later on rather than simply let it go.

Why not instead simply allow the driver to have his accident somewhere else? Try to have compassion for the person and remember how painful it is to be in such an enormous hurry. This way, we can maintain our own sense of well-being and avoid taking other people's problems personally.

There are many similar, "small stuff" examples that occur every day in our lives. Whether we had to wait in line, listen to unfair criticism, or do the lion's share of the work, it pays enormous dividends if we learn not to worry about little things. So many people spend so much of their life energy "sweating the small stuff" that they completely lose touch with the magic and beauty of life. When you commit to working toward this goal you will find that you will have far more energy to be kinder and gentler.

Make Peace with Imperfection

I've yet to meet an absolute perfectionist whose life was filled with inner peace. The need for perfection and the desire for inner tranquility conflict with each other. Whenever we are attached to having something a certain way, better than it already is, we are, almost by definition, engaged in a losing battle. Rather than being content and grateful for what we have, we are focused on what's wrong with something and our need to fix it. When we are zeroed in on what's wrong, it implies that we are dissatisfied, discontent.

Whether it's related to ourselves—a disorganized closet, a scratch on the car, an imperfect accomplishment, a few pounds we would like to lose—or someone else's "imperfections"—the way someone looks, behaves, or lives their life—the very act of focusing on imperfection pulls us away from our goal of being kind and gentle. This strategy has nothing to do with ceasing to do your very best but with being overly attached and focused on what's wrong with life. It's about realizing that while there's always a better way to do something, this doesn't mean that you can't enjoy and appreciate the way things already are.

The solution here is to catch yourself when you fall into your habit of insisting that things should be other than they are. Gently remind yourself that life is okay the way it is, right now. In the absence of your judgment, everything would be fine. As you begin to eliminate your need for perfection in all areas of your life, you'll begin to discover the perfection in life itself.

Be Aware of the Snowball Effect
of Your Thinking

A powerful technique for becoming more peaceful is to be aware of how quickly your negative and insecure thinking can spiral out of control. Have you ever noticed how uptight you feel when you're caught up in your thinking? And, to top it off, the more absorbed you get in the details of whatever is upsetting you, the worse you feel. One thought leads to another, and yet another, until at some point, you become incredibly agitated.

For example, you might wake up in the middle of the night and remember a phone call that needs to be made the following day. Then, rather than feeling relieved that you remembered such an important call, you start thinking about everything else you have to do tomorrow. You start rehearsing a probable conversation with your boss, getting yourself even more upset. Pretty soon you think to yourself, "I can't believe how busy I am. I must make fifty phone calls a day. Whose life is this anyway?" and on and on it goes until you're feeling sorry for yourself. For many people, there's no limit to how long this type of "thought attack" can go on. In fact, I've been told by clients that many of their days and nights are spent in this type of mental rehearsal. Needless to say, it's impossible to feel peaceful with your head full of concerns and annoyances.

The solution is to notice what's happening in your head before your thoughts have a chance to build any momentum. The sooner you catch yourself in the act of building your mental snowball, the easier it is to stop. In our example here, you might notice your snowball thinking right when you start running through the list of what you have to do the next day. Then, instead of obsessing on your upcoming day, you say to yourself, "Whew, there I go again," and consciously nip it in the bud. You stop your train of thought before it has a chance to get going. You can then focus, not on how overwhelmed you are, but on how grateful you are for remembering the phone call that needed to be made. If it's the middle of the night, write it down on a piece of paper and go back to sleep. You might even consider keeping a pen and paper by the bed for such moments.

You may indeed be a very busy person, but remember that filling your head with thoughts of how overwhelmed you are only exacerbates the problem by making you feel even more stressed than you already do. Try this simple little exercise the next time you begin to obsess on your schedule. You'll be amazed at how effective it can be.

Remind Yourself That When You Die, Your "In Basket" Won't Be Empty

So many of us live our lives as if the secret purpose is to somehow get everything done. We stay up late, get up early, avoid having fun, and keep our loved ones waiting. Sadly, I've seen many people who put off their loved ones so long that the loved ones lose interest in maintaining the relationship. I used to do this myself. Often, we convince ourselves that our obsession with our "to do" list is only temporary—that once we get through the list, we'll be calm, relaxed, and happy. But in reality, this rarely happens. As items are checked off, new ones simply replace them.

The nature of your "in basket" is that it's *meant* to have items to be completed in it—it's not meant to be empty. There will always be phone calls that need to be made, projects to complete, and work to be done. In fact, it can be argued that a full "in basket" is essential for success. It means your time is in demand!

Regardless of who you are or what you do, however, remember that *nothing* is more important than your own sense of happiness and inner peace and that of your loved ones. If you're obsessed with getting everything done, you'll never have a sense of well-being! In reality, almost everything can wait. Very little in our work lives truly falls into the "emergency" category. If you stay focused on your work, it will all get done in due time.

I find that if I remind myself (frequently) that the purpose of life *isn't* to get it all done but to enjoy each step along the way and live a life filled with love, it's far easier for me to control my obsession with completing my list of things to do. Remember, when you die, there *will* still be unfinished business to take care of. And you know what? Someone else will do it for you! Don't waste any more precious moments of your life regretting the inevitable.

Do Something Nice for Someone Else— and Don't Tell *Anyone* About It

While many of us frequently do nice things for others, we are almost certain to mention our acts of kindness to someone else, secretly seeking their approval.

When we share our own niceness or generosity with someone else, it makes us feel like we are thoughtful people, it reminds us of how nice we are and how deserving we are of kindness.

While all acts of kindness are inherently wonderful, there is something even more magical about doing something thoughtful but mentioning it to no one, ever. You always feel good when you give to others. Rather than diluting the positive feelings by telling others about your own kindness, by keeping it to yourself you get to retain *all* the positive feelings.

It's really true that one should give for the sake of giving, not to receive something in return. This is precisely what you are doing when you don't mention your kindness to others—your rewards are the warm feelings that come from the act of giving. The next time you do something really nice for someone else, keep it to yourself and revel in the abundant joy of giving.

Let Others Have the Glory

There is something magical that happens to the human spirit, a sense of calm that comes over you, when you cease needing all the attention directed toward yourself and instead allow others to have the glory.

Our need for excessive attention is that ego-centered part of us that says, "Look at me. I'm special. My story is more interesting than yours." It's that voice inside of us that may not come right out and say it, but that wants to believe that "my accomplishments are slightly more important than yours." The ego is that part of us that wants to be seen, heard, respected, considered special, often at the expense of someone else. It's the part of us that interrupts someone else's story, or impatiently waits his turn to speak so that he can bring the conversation and attention back to himself. To varying degrees, most of us engage in this habit, much to our own detriment. When you immediately dive in and bring the conversation back toward you, you can subtly minimize the joy that person has in sharing, and in doing so, create distance between yourself and others. Everyone loses.

The next time someone tells you a story or shares an accomplishment with you, notice your tendency to say something about yourself in response.

Although it's a difficult habit to break, it's not only enjoyable but actually peaceful to have the quiet confidence to be able to surrender your need for attention and instead share in the joy of someone else's glory. Rather than jumping right in and saying, "Once I did the same thing" or "Guess what I did today," bite your tongue and notice what happens. Just say, "That's wonderful," or "Please tell me more," and leave it at that. The person you are speaking to will have so much more fun and, because you are so much more "present," because you are listening so carefully, he or she won't feel in competition with you. The result will be that the person will feel more relaxed around you, making him or her more confident as well as more interesting. You too will feel more relaxed because you won't be on the edge of your seat, waiting your turn.

Obviously, there are many times when it's absolutely appropriate to exchange experience back and forth, and to share *in* the glory and attention rather than giving it all away. I'm referring here to the compulsive need to grab it from others. Ironically, when you surrender your need to hog the glory, the attention you used to need from other people is replaced by a quiet inner confidence that is derived from letting others have it.

Learn to Live in the Present Moment

To a large degree, the measure of our peace of mind is determined by how much we are able to live in the present moment. Irrespective of what happened yesterday or last year, and what may or may not happen tomorrow, the present moment is where you are—always!

Without question, many of us have mastered the neurotic art of spending much of our lives worrying about a variety of things—all at once. We allow past problems and future concerns to dominate our present moments, so much so that we end up anxious, frustrated, depressed, and hopeless. On the flip side, we also postpone our gratification, our stated priorities, and our happiness, often convincing ourselves that "someday" will be better than today. Unfortunately, the same mental dynamics that tell us to look toward the future will only repeat themselves so that "someday" never actually arrives. John Lennon once said, "Life is what's happening while we're busy making other plans." When we're busy making "other plans," our children are busy growing up, the people we love are moving away and dying, our bodies are getting out of shape, and our dreams are slipping away. In short, we miss out on life.

Many people live as if life were a dress rehearsal for some later date. It isn't. In fact, no one has a guarantee that he or she will be here tomorrow. Now is the only time we have, and the only time that we have any control over. When our attention is in the present moment, we push fear from our minds. Fear is the concern over events that might happen in the future—we won't have enough money, our children will get into trouble, we will get old and die, whatever.

To combat fear, the best strategy is to learn to bring your attention back to the present. Mark Twain said, "I have been through some terrible things in my life, some of which actually happened." I don't think I can say it any better. Practice keeping your attention on the here and now. Your efforts will pay great dividends.

Ask Yourself the Question, "Will This Matter a Year from Now?"

Almost every day I play a game with myself that I call "time warp." I made it up in response to my consistent, erroneous belief that what I was all worked up about was really important.

To play "time warp," all you have to do is imagine that whatever circumstance you are dealing with isn't happening right now but a year from now. Then simply ask yourself, "Is this situation really as important as I'm making it out to be?" Once in a great while it may be—but a vast majority of the time, it simply isn't.

Whether it be an argument with your spouse, child, or boss, a mistake, a lost opportunity, a lost wallet, a work-related rejection, or a sprained ankle, chances are, a year from now you aren't going to care. It will be one more irrelevant detail in your life. While this simple game won't solve all your problems, it can give you an enormous amount of needed perspective. I find myself laughing at things that I used to take far too seriously. Now, rather than using up my energy feeling angry and overwhelmed, I can use it instead on spending time with my wife and children or engaging in creative thinking.

≈ 9 ≈

Allow Yourself to Be Bored

For many of us, our lives are so filled with stimuli, not to mention responsibilities, that it's almost impossible for us to sit still and do nothing, much less relax—even for a few minutes. A friend of mine said to me, "People are no longer human beings. We should be called human doings."

I was first exposed to the idea that occasional boredom can actually be good for me while studying with a therapist in La Conner, Washington, a tiny little town with very little "to do." After finishing our first day together, I asked my instructor, "What is there to do around here at night?" He responded by saying, "What I'd like you to do is allow yourself to be bored. Do nothing. This is part of your training." At first I thought he was kidding! "Why on earth would I choose to be bored?" I asked. He went on to explain that if you allow yourself to be bored, even for an hour—or less—and don't fight it, the feelings of boredom will be replaced with feelings of peace. And after a little practice, you'll learn to relax.

Much to my surprise, he was absolutely right. At first, I could barely stand it. I was so used to doing something every second that I really struggled to relax. But after a while I got used to it, and have long since learned to enjoy it. I'm not talking about hours of idle time or laziness, but simply learning the art of relaxing, of just "being," rather than "doing," for a few minutes each day. There isn't a specific technique other than to consciously do nothing. Just sit still, perhaps look out the window and notice your thoughts and feelings. At first you may get a little anxious, but each day it will get a little easier. The payback is tremendous.

Much of our anxiety and inner struggle stems from our busy, overactive minds always needing something to entertain them, something to focus on, and always wondering "What's next?" While we're eating dinner we wonder what's for dessert. While eating dessert, we ponder what we should do afterward. After that evening, it's "What should we do this weekend?" After we've been out, we walk into the house and immediately turn on the television, pick up the phone, open a book, or start cleaning. It's almost as though we're frightened at the thought of not having something to do, even for a minute.

The beauty of doing nothing is that it teaches you to clear your mind and relax. It allows your mind the freedom to "not know," for a brief period of time. Just like your body, your mind needs an occasional break from its hectic routine. When you allow your mind to take a break, it comes back stronger, sharper, more focused and creative.

When you allow yourself to be bored, it takes an enormous amount of pressure off you to be performing and doing something every second of every day. Now, when either of my two children says to me, "Daddy, I'm bored," I respond by saying, "Great, be bored for a while. It's good for you." Once I say this, they always give up on the idea of me solving their problem. You probably never thought someone would actually suggest that you allow yourself to be bored. I guess there's a first for everything!

Once a Week, Write a Heartfelt Letter

This is an exercise that has helped to change many lives, assisting people in becoming more peaceful and loving. Taking a few minutes each week to write a heartfelt letter does many things for you. Picking up a pen or typing on a keyboard slows you down long enough to remember the beautiful people in your life. The act of sitting down to write helps to fill your life with gratitude.

Once you decide to try this, you'll probably be amazed at how many people appear on your list. I had one client who said, "I probably don't have enough weeks left in my life to write everyone on my list." This may or may not be true for you, but chances are, there are a number of people in your life, or from your past, who are quite deserving of a friendly, heartfelt letter. Even if you don't have people in your life to whom you feel you can write, go ahead and write the letter to someone you don't know instead—perhaps to an author who may not even be living, whose works you admire. Or to a great inventor or thinker from the past or present. Part of the value of the letter is to gear your thinking toward gratitude. Writing the letter, even if it isn't sent, would do just that.

The purpose of your letter is very simple: to express love and gratitude. Don't worry if you're awkward at writing letters. This isn't a contest from the head but a gift from the heart. If you can't think of much to say, start with short little notes like, "Dear Jasmine. I woke up this morning thinking of how lucky I am to have people like you in my life. Thank you so much for being my friend. I am truly blessed, and I wish for you all the happiness and joy that life can bring. Love, Richard."

Not only does writing and sending a note like this focus your attention on what's right in your life, but the person receiving it will, in all likelihood, be extremely touched and grateful. Often, this simple action starts a spiral of loving actions whereby the person receiving your letter may decide to do the same thing to someone else, or perhaps will act and feel more loving toward others. Write your first letter this week. I'll bet you'll be glad you did.

Repeat to Yourself,
"Life Isn't an Emergency"

In some ways, this strategy epitomizes the essential message of this book. Although most people believe otherwise, the truth is, life *isn't* an emergency.

I've had hundreds of clients over the years who have all but neglected their families as well as their own dreams because of their propensity to believe that life is an emergency. They justify their neurotic behavior by believing that if they don't work eighty hours a week, they won't get everything done. Sometimes I remind them that when they die, their "in basket" won't be empty!

A client who is a homemaker and mother of three children recently said to me, "I just can't get the house cleaned up the way I like it before everyone leaves in the morning." She was so upset over her inability to be perfect that her doctor had prescribed her anti-anxiety medicine. She was acting (and feeling) like there was a gun pointed at her head and the sniper was demanding that every dish be put away and every towel folded—or else! Again, the silent assumption was, *this is an emergency!* The truth was, no one other than she had created the pressure she was experiencing.

I've never met anyone (myself included) who hasn't turned little things into great big emergencies. We take our own goals so seriously that we forget to have fun along the way, and we forget to cut ourselves some slack. We take simple preferences and turn them into conditions for our own happiness. Or, we beat ourselves up if we can't meet our self-created deadlines. The first step in becoming a more peaceful person is to have the humility to admit that, in most cases, you're creating your own emergencies. Life will usually go on if things don't go according to plan. It's helpful to keep reminding yourself and repeating the sentence, "Life isn't an emergency."

Imagine the People in Your Life as Tiny Infants and as One-Hundred-Year-Old Adults

I learned this technique almost twenty years ago. It has proven to be extremely successful for releasing feelings of irritation toward other people.

Think of someone who truly irritates you, who makes you feel angry. Now, close your eyes and try to imagine this person as a tiny infant. See their tiny little features and their innocent little eyes. Know that babies can't help but make mistakes and each of us was, at one time, a little infant. Now, roll forward the clock one hundred years. See the same person as a very old person who is about to die. Look at their worn-out eyes and their soft smile, which suggests a bit of wisdom and the admission of mistakes made. Know that each of us will be one hundred years old, alive or dead, before too many decades go by.

You can play with this technique and alter it in many ways. It almost always provides the user with some needed perspective and compassion. If our goal is to become more peaceful and loving, we certainly don't want to harbor negativity toward others.

Become a Better Listener

I grew up believing I was a good listener. And although I have become a better listener than I was ten years ago, I have to admit I'm still only an *adequate* listener.

Effective listening is more than simply avoiding the bad habit of interrupting others while they are speaking or finishing their sentences. It's being content to listen to the *entire* thought of someone rather than waiting impatiently for your chance to respond.

In some ways, the way we fail to listen is symbolic of the way we live. We often treat communication as if it were a race. It's almost like our goal is to have no time gaps between the conclusion of the sentence of the person we are speaking with and the beginning of our own. My wife and I were recently at a café having lunch, eavesdropping on the conversations around us. It seemed that no one was really listening to one another; instead they were taking turns not listening to one another. I asked my wife if I still did the same thing. With a smile on her face she said, "Only sometimes."

Slowing down your responses and becoming a better listener aids you in becoming a more peaceful person. It takes pressure from you. If you think about it, you'll notice that it takes an enormous amount of energy and is very stressful to be sitting at the edge of your seat trying to guess what the person in front of you (or on the telephone) is going to say so that you can fire back your response. But as you wait for the people you are communicating with to finish, as you simply listen more intently to what is being said, you'll notice that the pressure you feel is off. You'll immediately feel more relaxed, and so will the people you are talking to. They will feel safe in slowing down their own responses because they won't feel in competition with you for "airtime"! Not only will becoming a better listener make you a more patient person, it will also enhance the quality of your relationships. Everyone loves to talk to someone who truly listens to what they are saying.

Choose Your Battles Wisely

"Choose your battles wisely" is a popular phrase in parenting but is equally important in living a contented life. It suggests that life is filled with opportunities to choose between making a big deal out of something or simply letting it go, realizing it doesn't really matter. If you choose your battles wisely, you'll be far more effective in winning those that are truly important.

Certainly there will be times when you will want or need to argue, confront, or even fight for something you believe in. Many people, however, argue, confront, and fight over practically anything, turning their lives into a series of battles over relatively "small stuff." There is so much frustration in living this type of life that you lose track of what is truly relevant.

The tiniest disagreement or glitch in your plans can be made into a big deal if your goal (conscious or unconscious) is to have everything work out in your favor. In my book, this is nothing more than a prescription for unhappiness and frustration.

The truth is, life is rarely exactly the way we want it to be, and other people often don't act as we would like them to. Moment to moment, there are aspects of life that we like and others that we don't. There are always going to be people who disagree with you, people who do things differently, and things that don't work out. If you fight against this principle of life, you'll spend most of your life fighting battles.

A more peaceful way to live is to decide consciously which battles are worth fighting and which are better left alone. If your primary goal isn't to have everything work out perfectly but instead to live a relatively stress-free life, you'll find that most battles pull you *away from* your most tranquil feelings. Is it really important that you prove to your spouse that you are right and she is wrong, or that you confront someone simply because it appears as though he or she has made a minor mistake? Does your preference of which restaurant or movie to go to matter enough to argue over it? Does a small scratch on your car really warrant a suit in small claims court? Does the fact that your neighbor won't park his car on a different part of the street have to be discussed at your family dinner table? These and thousands of other small things are what many people spend their lives fighting about. Take a look at your own list. If it's like mine used to be, you might want to reevaluate your priorities.

If you don't want to "sweat the small stuff," it's critical that you choose your battles wisely. If you do, there will come a day when you'll rarely feel the need to do battle at all.

Praise and Blame Are All the Same

One of the most unavoidable life lessons is having to deal with the disapproval of others. Praise and blame are all the same is a fancy way of reminding yourself of the old cliché that you'll never be able to please all the people all the time. Even in a landslide election victory in which a candidate secures 55 percent of the vote, he or she is left with 45 percent of the population that wishes someone else were the winner. Pretty humbling, isn't it?

Our approval rating from family, friends, and the people we work with isn't likely to be much higher. The truth is, everyone has their own set of ideas with which to evaluate life, and our ideas don't always match those of other people. For some reason, however, most of us struggle against this inevitable fact. We get angry, hurt, or otherwise frustrated when people reject our ideas, tell us no, or give us some other form of disapproval.

The sooner we accept the inevitable dilemma of not being able to win the approval of everyone we meet, the easier our lives will become. When you expect to be dished out your share of disapproval instead of struggling against this fact, you'll develop a helpful perspective to assist your life journey. Rather than feeling rejected by disapproval, you can remind yourself, "Here it is again. That's okay

You can learn to be pleasantly surprised, even grateful when you receive the approval you're hoping for.

I find that there are many days when I experience both praise and blame. Someone will hire me to speak and someone else won't want to; one phone call delivers good news, another announces a new issue to deal with. One of my children is happy with my behavior, the other struggles against it. Someone says what a nice guy I am, someone else thinks I'm selfish because I don't return his phone call. This back and forth, good and bad, approval and disapproval is a part of everyone's life. I'm the first to admit that I always prefer approval over disapproval. It feels better and it's certainly easier to deal with. The more content I've become, however, the less I depend on it for my sense of well-being.

See the Innocence

For many people, one of the most frustrating aspects of life is not being able to understand other people's behavior. We see them as "guilty" instead of "innocent." It's tempting to focus on people's seemingly irrational behavior—their comments, actions, mean-spirited acts, selfish behavior—and get extremely frustrated. If we focus on behavior too much, it can seem like other people are making us miserable.

But as I once heard Wayne Dyer sarcastically suggest in a lecture, "Round up all the people who are making you miserable and bring them to me. I will treat them [as a counselor], and you'll get better!" Obviously, this is absurd. It's true that other people do weird things (who doesn't?), but *we* are the ones getting upset, so we are the ones who need to change. I'm not talking about accepting, ignoring, or advocating violence or any other deviant behavior. I'm merely talking about learning to be less *bothered* by the actions of people.

Seeing the innocence is a powerful tool for transformation that means when someone is acting in a way that we don't like, the best strategy for dealing with that person is to distance ourselves from the behavior; to "look beyond it," so that we can see the innocence in where the behavior is coming from. Very often, this slight shift in our thinking immediately puts us into a state of compassion.

Occasionally, I work with people who are pressuring me to hurry up. Often, their technique for getting me to hurry along is obnoxious, even insulting. If I focus on the words they use, the tone of their voices, and the urgency of their messages, I can get annoyed, even angry in my responses. I see them as "guilty." However, if I remember the urgency *I* feel when I'm in a hurry to do something, it allows me to see the innocence in their behavior. Underneath even the most annoying behavior is a frustrated person who is crying out for compassion.

The next time (and hopefully from now on), when someone acts in a strange way, look for the innocence in his behavior. If you're compassionate, it won't be hard to see. When you see the innocence, the same things that have always frustrated you no longer do. And, when you're not frustrated by the actions of others, it's a lot easier to stay focused on the beauty of life.

Resist the Urge to Criticize

When we judge or criticize another person, it says nothing about that person; it merely says something about our own need to be critical.

If you attend a gathering and listen to all the criticism that is typically levied against others, and then go home and consider how much good all that criticism actually does to make our world a better place, you'll probably come up with the same answer that I do: Zero! It does no good. But that's not all. Being critical not only solves nothing; it contributes to the anger and distrust in our world. After all, none of us likes to be criticized. Our reaction to criticism is usually to become defensive and/or withdrawn. A person who feels attacked is likely to do one of two things: he will either retreat in fear or shame, or he will attack or lash out in anger. How many times have you criticized someone and had them respond by saying, "Thank you so much for pointing out my flaws. I really appreciate it"?

Criticism, like swearing, is actually nothing more than a bad habit. It's something we get used to doing; we're familiar with how it feels. It keeps us busy and gives us something to talk about.

If, however, you take a moment to observe how you actually feel immediately after you criticize someone, you'll notice that you will feel a little deflated and ashamed, almost like *you're* the one who has been attacked. The reason this is true is that when we criticize, it's a statement to the world and to ourselves, "I have a need to be critical." This isn't something we are usually proud to admit.

The solution is to catch yourself in the act of being critical. Notice how often you do it and how bad it makes you feel. What I like to do is turn it into a game. I still catch myself being critical, but as my need to criticize arises, I try to remember to say to myself, "There I go again." Hopefully, more often than not, I can turn my criticism into tolerance and respect.

Search for the Grain of Truth in Other Opinions

If you enjoy learning as well as making other people happy, you'll love this idea.

Almost everyone feels that their own opinions are good ones, otherwise they wouldn't be sharing them with you. One of the destructive things that many of us do, however, is compare someone else's opinion to our own. And, when it doesn't fall in line with our belief, we either dismiss it or find fault with it. We feel smug, the other person feels diminished, and we learn nothing.

Almost every opinion has some merit, especially if we are looking for merit, rather than looking for errors. The next time someone offers you an opinion, rather than judge or criticize it, see if you can find a grain of truth in what the person is saying.

If you think about it, when you judge someone else or their opinion, it really doesn't say *anything* about the other person, but it says quite a bit about your need to be judgmental.

I still catch myself criticizing other points of view, but far less than I used to. All that changed was my intention to find the grain of truth in other positions. If you practice this simple strategy, some wonderful things will begin to happen: You'll begin to understand those you interact with, others will be drawn to your accepting and loving energy, your learning curve will be enhanced, and, perhaps most important, you'll feel much better about yourself.

Become a Less Aggressive Driver

Where do you get the most uptight? If you're like most people, driving in traffic is probably high on your list. To look at most major freeways these days, you'd think you were on a racetrack instead of a roadway.

There are three excellent reasons for becoming a less aggressive driver. First, when you are aggressive, you put yourself and everyone around you in extreme danger. Second, driving aggressively is extremely stressful. Your blood pressure goes up, your grip on the wheel tightens, your eyes are strained, and your thoughts are spinning out of control. Finally, you end up saving no time in getting to where you want to go.

Recently I was driving south from Oakland to San Jose. Traffic was heavy, but moving. I noticed an extremely aggressive and angry driver weaving in and out of the lanes, speeding up and slowing down. Clearly, he was in a hurry. For the most part I remained in the same lane for the entire forty-mile journey. I was listening to a new audiotape I had just purchased and daydreaming along the way. I enjoyed the trip a great deal because driving gives me a chance to be alone. As I was exiting off the freeway, the aggressive driver came up behind me and raced on by. Without realizing it, I had actually arrived in San Jose ahead of him. All of his weaving, rapid acceleration, and putting families at risk had earned him nothing except perhaps some high blood pressure and a great deal of wear and tear on his vehicle. On average, he and I had driven at the same speed.

The same principle applies when you see drivers speeding past you so that they can beat you to the next stoplight. It simply doesn't pay to speed. This is especially true if you get a ticket and have to spend eight hours in traffic school. It will take you years of dangerous speeding to make up this time alone.

When you make the conscious decision to become a less aggressive driver, you begin using your time in the car to relax. Try to see your driving not only as a way of getting you somewhere, but as a chance to breathe and to reflect. Rather than tensing your muscles, see if you can relax them instead. I even have a few audiotapes that are specifically geared toward muscular relaxation. Sometimes I pop one in and listen. By the time I reach my destination I feel more relaxed than I did before getting into the car. During the course of your lifetime, you're probably going to spend a great deal of time driving. You can spend those moments being frustrated, or you can use them wisely. If you do the latter, you'll be a more relaxed person.

20

Turn Your Melodrama
into a Mellow-Drama

In a certain respect, this strategy is just another way of saying, "Don't sweat the small stuff." Many people live as if life were a melodrama— "an extravagantly theatrical play in which action and plot predominate." Sound familiar? In dramatic fashion, we blow things out of proportion, and make a big deal out of little things. We forget that life isn't as bad as we're making it out to be. We also forget that when we're blowing things out of proportion, *we* are the ones doing the blowing.

I've found that simply reminding myself that life doesn't have to be a soap opera is a powerful method of calming down. When I get too worked up or start taking myself too seriously (which happens more than I like to admit), I say to myself something like, "Here I go again. My soap opera is starting." Almost always, this takes the edge off my seriousness and helps me laugh at myself. Often, this simple reminder enables me to change the channel to a more peaceful station. My melodrama is transformed into a "mellow-drama."

If you've ever watched a soap opera, you've seen how the characters will take little things so seriously as to ruin their lives over them— someone says something to offend them, looks at them wrong, or flirts with their spouse. Their response is usually, "Oh my gosh. How could this happen to me?" Then they exacerbate the problem by talking to others about "how awful it is." They turn life into an emergency—a melodrama.

The next time you feel stressed out, experiment with this strategy—remind yourself that life isn't an emergency and turn your melodrama into a mellow-drama.

21

Think of What You Have
Instead of What You Want

In over a dozen years as a stress consultant, one of the most pervasive and destructive mental tendencies I've seen is that of focusing on what we *want* instead of what we *have*. It doesn't seem to make any difference how much we have; we just keep expanding our list of desires, which guarantees we will remain dissatisfied. The mind-set that says "I'll be happy when this desire is fulfilled" is the same mind-set that will repeat itself once that desire is met.

A friend of ours closed escrow on his new home on a Sunday. The very next time we saw him he was talking about his next house that was going to be even bigger! He isn't alone. Most of us do the very same thing. We want this or that. If we don't get what we want we keep thinking about all that we don't have—and we remain dissatisfied. If we do get what we want, we simply re-create the same thinking in our new circumstances. So, despite getting what we want, we still remain unhappy. Happiness can't be found when we are yearning for new desires.

Luckily, there is a way to be happy. It involves changing the emphasis of our thinking from what we want to what we have. Rather than wishing your spouse were different, try thinking about her wonderful qualities. Instead of complaining about your salary, be grateful that you have a job. Rather than wishing you were able to take a vacation to Hawaii, think of how much fun you have had close to home. The list of possibilities is endless! Each time you notice yourself falling into the "I wish life were different" trap, back off and start over. Take a breath and remember all that you have to be grateful for. When you focus not on what you want, but on what you have, you end up getting more of what you want anyway. If you focus on the good qualities of your spouse, she'll be more loving. If you are grateful for your job rather than complaining about it, you'll do a better job, be more productive, and probably end up getting a raise anyway. If you focus on ways to enjoy yourself around home rather than waiting to enjoy yourself in Hawaii, you'll end up having more fun. If you ever do get to Hawaii, you'll be in the habit of enjoying yourself. And, if by some chance you don't, you'll have a great life anyway.

Make a note to yourself to start thinking more about what you have than what you want. If you do, your life will start appearing much better than before. For perhaps the first time in your life, you'll know what it means to feel satisfied.

22

Stop Blaming Others

When something doesn't meet our expectations, many of us operate with the assumption, "When in doubt, it must be someone else's fault." You can see this assumption in action almost everywhere you look—something is missing, so someone else must have moved it; the car isn't working right, so the mechanic must have repaired it incorrectly; your expenses exceed your income, so your spouse must be spending too much money; the house is a mess, so you must be the only person doing your part; a project is late, so your colleagues at work must not have done their share—and on and on it goes.

This type of blaming thinking has become extremely common in our culture. On a personal level, it has led us to believe that we are never completely responsible for our own actions, problems, or happiness. On a societal level, it has led to frivolous lawsuits and ridiculous excuses that get criminals off the hook. When we are in the habit of blaming others, we will blame others for our anger, frustration, depression, stress, and unhappiness.

In terms of personal happiness, you *cannot* be peaceful while at the same time blaming others. Surely there are times when other people and/or circumstances contribute to our problems, but it is we who must rise to the occasion and take responsibility for our own happiness. Circumstances don't make a person, they reveal him or her.

As an experiment, notice what happens when you stop blaming others for anything and everything in your life. This doesn't mean you don't hold people accountable for their actions, but that you hold *yourself* accountable for your own happiness and for your reactions to other people and the circumstances around you. When the house is a mess, rather than assuming you're the only person doing your part, clean it up! When you're over budget, figure out where *you* can spend less money. Most important, when you're unhappy, remind yourself that only you can make yourself happy.

Blaming others takes an enormous amount of mental energy. It's a "drag-me-down" mind-set that creates stress and disease. Blaming makes you feel powerless over your own life because your happiness is contingent on the actions and behavior of others, which you can't control. When you stop blaming others, you will regain your sense of personal power. You will see yourself as a choice maker. You will know that when you are upset, you are playing a key role in the creation of your own feelings. This means that you can also play a key role in creating new, more positive feelings. Life is a great deal more fun and much easier to manage when you stop blaming others. Give it a try and see what happens.

23

Transform Your Relationship
to Your Problems

Obstacles and problems are a part of life. True happiness comes not when we get rid of all of our problems, but when we change our relationship to them, when we see our problems as a potential source of awakening, opportunities to practice patience and to learn. Perhaps the most basic principle of spiritual life is that our problems are the best places to practice keeping our hearts open.

Certainly some problems need to be solved. Many others, however, are problems we create for ourselves by struggling to make our life different than it actually is. Inner peace is accomplished by understanding and accepting the inevitable contradictions of life—the pain and pleasure, success and failure, joy and sorrow, births and deaths. Problems can teach us to be gracious, humble, and patient.

In the Buddhist tradition, difficulties are considered to be so important to a life of growth and peace that a Tibetan prayer actually asks for them. It says, "Grant that I may be given appropriate difficulties and sufferings on this journey so that my heart may be truly awakened and my practice of liberation and universal compassion may be truly fulfilled." It is felt that when life is too easy, there are fewer opportunities for genuine growth.

I wouldn't go so far as to recommend that you seek out problems. I would, however, suggest that if you spend less time running away from problems and trying to rid yourself of them—and more time accepting problems as an inevitable, natural, even important part of life—you will soon discover that life can be more of a dance and less of a battle. This philosophy of acceptance is the root of going with the flow.

24

If Someone Throws You the Ball, You Don't Have to Catch It

My best friend, Benjamin Shield, taught me this valuable lesson. Often our inner struggles come from our tendency to jump on board someone else's problem; someone throws you a concern and you assume you must catch it, and respond. For example, suppose you're really busy when a friend calls in a frantic tone and says, "My mother is driving me crazy. What should I do?" Rather than saying, "I'm really sorry but I don't know what to suggest," you automatically catch the ball and try to solve the problem. Then later, you feel stressed or resentful that you are behind schedule and that everyone seems to be making demands on you. It's easy to lose sight of your willing participation in the dramas of your own life.

Remembering that you don't have to catch the ball is a very effective way to reduce the stress in your life. When your friend calls, you *can* drop the ball, meaning you don't have to participate simply because he or she is attempting to lure you in. If you don't take the bait, the person will probably call someone else to see if they will become involved.

This doesn't mean you never catch the ball, only that it's your choice to do so. Neither does this mean that you don't care about your friend, or that you're crass or unhelpful. Developing a more tranquil outlook on life requires that we know our own limits and that we take responsibility for our part in the process. Most of us get balls thrown at us many times each day—at work, from our children, friends, neighbors, salespeople, even strangers. If I caught all the balls thrown in my direction, I would certainly go crazy—and I suspect that you would too! The key is to know when we're catching another ball so that we won't feel victimized, resentful, or overwhelmed.

Even something terribly simple like answering your phone when you're really too busy to talk is a form of catching the ball. By answering the phone, you are willingly taking part in an interaction that you may not have the time, energy, or mind-set for at the present time. By simply not answering the phone, you are taking responsibility for your own peace of mind. The same idea applies to being insulted or criticized. When someone throws an idea or comment in your direction, you can catch it and feel hurt, or you can drop it and go on with your day.

The idea of "not catching the ball" simply because it's thrown to you is a powerful tool to explore. I hope you'll experiment with this one. You may find that you catch the ball a lot more than you think you do.

~ℰ 25 ℰ~

Mind Your Own Business

It's tough enough trying to create a life of serenity when dealing with your own mental tendencies, issues, real-life problems, habits, and the contradictions and complexities of life. But when you feel compelled to deal with other people's issues, your goal of becoming more peaceful becomes all but impossible.

How often do you find yourself saying things like, "I wouldn't do that if I were her," or "I can't believe he did that," or "What is she thinking about?" How often are you frustrated, bothered, annoyed, or concerned about things that you not only *cannot* control or be of actual help with, but are also none of your business?

This is not a prescription to avoid being of help to people. Rather, it's about knowing when to help and when to leave something alone. I used to be the type of person who would jump in and try to solve a problem without being asked. Not only did my efforts prove fruitless, they were also almost always unappreciated, and sometimes even resented. Since recovering from my need to be overly involved, my life has become much simpler. And, now that I'm not butting in where I'm not wanted, I'm far more available to be of help when I am asked or truly needed.

Minding your own business goes far beyond simply avoiding the temptation to try to solve other people's problems. It also includes

46

eavesdropping, gossiping, talking behind other people's backs, and analyzing or trying to figure out other people. One of the major reasons most of us focus on the shortcomings or problems of others is to avoid looking at ourselves.

When you catch yourself involved where you really don't belong, congratulate yourself for having the humility and wisdom to back off. In no time at all, you'll free up tons of extra energy to focus your attention where it's truly relevant or needed.

26

Live This Day as if It Were Your Last.
It Might Be!

When are you going to die? In fifty years, twenty, ten, five, today? Last time I checked, no one had told me. I often wonder, when listening to the news, did the person who died in the auto accident on his way home from work remember to tell his family how much he loved them? Did he live well? Did he love well? Perhaps the only thing that is certain is that he still had things in his "in basket" that weren't yet done.

The truth is, none of us has any idea how long we have to live. Sadly, however, we act as if we're going to live forever. We postpone the things that, deep down, we know we want to do—telling the people we love how much we care, spending time alone, visiting a good friend, taking that beautiful hike, running a marathon, writing a heartfelt letter, going fishing with your daughter, learning to meditate, becoming a better listener, and on and on. We come up with elaborate and sophisticated rationales to justify our actions, and end up spending most of our time and energy doing things that aren't all that important. We argue for our limitations, and they become our limitations.

I felt it appropriate to end this section of the book by suggesting that you live each day as if it were your last on this earth. I suggest this not as a prescription to be reckless or to abandon your responsibilities, but to remind you of how precious life really is. A friend of mine once said, "Life is too important to take too seriously." Ten years later, I know he was right. I hope that this section has been, and will continue to be, helpful to you. Please don't forget the most basic strategy of all, *Don't sweat the small stuff!* I will end this section by sincerely saying that I wish you well.

Treasure yourself.

DON'T SWEAT THE SMALL STUFF AT WORK

27

Dare to Be Happy

Many people don't allow themselves the luxury of being enthusiastic, light-hearted, inspired, relaxed, or happy—especially at work. To me, this is a very unfortunate form of self-denial. It seems that a great number of people are frightened at what a happy demeanor would look like to other people, including coworkers, clients, and employers. After all, they assume, "Someone who is relaxed (or happy) must not be a hard worker." The logic goes something like this: If they looked happy, others might assume they were satisfied with the status quo and therefore lacking the necessary motivation to excel in their work or go the extra mile. They certainly couldn't survive in a competitive environment.

I'm often hired to speak to corporations around the country on stress reduction and happier living. On a number of occasions, the person who invited me to speak has asked me, in a nervous tone, whether I would help the employees become so happy that they would "lose their edge." I'm not kidding!

In reality, it's the other way around. It's nonsense to believe that a relaxed, happy person necessarily lacks motivation. On the contrary, happy people are almost always the ones who love what they do. It's been shown again and again that people who love what they do are highly motivated by their own enthusiasm to continually better themselves and their performance. They are good listeners and have a sharp learning curve. In addition, happy workers are highly creative, charismatic, easy to be around, and good team players.

Unhappy people, on the other hand, are often held back by their own misery or stress, which distracts them from success. Rigid, stressed-out people are a drag to be around and difficult to work with. They are the ones who lack motivation because they are so consumed with their own problems, lack of time, and stress. Unhappy people often feel victimized by others and their working conditions. It's difficult for them to be solution-oriented because everything is seen as someone else's fault. In addition, they are usually poor team players because they are often self-centered and preoccupied with their own issues. They are defensive and, almost always, poor listeners. If they are successful, it's despite their unhappiness, not because of it. In fact, if an unhappy, stressed-out person can learn to become happier, he or she will become even more successful.

I felt this strategy would be an excellent way to introduce this section of the book because one of my goals is to convince you that *it's okay to be happy, kind, patient, more relaxed and forgiving.* It's to your advantage, personally and professionally. You won't lose your edge, nor will you be "walked on." I can assure you that you won't become apathetic, uncaring, or unmotivated. To the contrary, you'll feel more inspired, creative, and driven to make an even greater contribution than you do right now. You'll see solutions and opportunities where others see problems. Likewise, rather than being discouraged by setbacks or failures, you'll bounce back quickly and resiliently. You will have increased energy, you'll be able to work "in the eye of the storm," and, because you'll be so level-headed, you'll be the one who is looked to when tough decisions need to be made. You will rise to the top.

If you dare to be happy, your life will begin to change immediately. Your life and your work will take on greater significance and will be experienced as an extraordinary adventure. You'll be loved by others and, without a doubt, you'll be sweating the small stuff far less often at work.

Become Less Controlling

When I talk about being "controlling," I'm referring to unhealthy attempts to manipulate the behavior of others, having the need to control your environment, insisting on having things be "just so" in order to feel secure, and becoming immobilized, defensive, or anxious when other people don't behave to your specifications—the way you think they should be. To be controlling means you are preoccupied with the actions of others and how those actions affect you. To put it in the context of this book, people who are controlling "sweat the behavior" of others when it doesn't match their own expectations.

I've made several observations about people who are controlling; two in particular. First, there are too many of them. For whatever reason, there seems to be a national trend toward controlling behavior. Secondly, the trait of being controlling is highly stressful—both to the controller and to those who are being controlled. If you want a more peaceful life, it's essential you become less controlling.

One of the most extreme examples of controlling behavior I've heard of involved, of all things, paper clips! A lawyer at a top-flight law firm had a penchant for certain things to be done in certain ways—not only "big picture" things, but very minuscule things as well. This fellow liked to use copper-colored paper clips instead of the silver ones his firm provided (what could be more important than that?). So he had his secretary buy his own private supply for him each week (and didn't even reimburse her). If something came to his desk with the wrong kind of clip, he'd fly into a rage. He became known in the office as "the paper clip king."

It probably won't come as a big surprise that this guy was almost always behind on his paperwork, and his work for his clients suffered. All the time he spent getting angry over petty things slowed him down. The paper clips were only one aspect of his controlling behavior—he had rules and regulations about everything from how his coffee was served (in a special china cup and saucer) to the order in which he was introduced in meetings. Ultimately, his controlling behavior turned off one too many of his clients, and he was let go from the firm.

This is a very unusual and extreme example, yet if you examine your own behavior, you may find areas that you are trying to control that are futile or just plain silly. I encourage you to take a look.

A person who is controlling carries with him a great deal of stress because, not only does he (or she) have to be concerned with his own choices and behavior, but in addition, he insists that others think and behave in certain ways as well. While occasionally we can influence another person, we certainly can't force him to be a certain way. To someone who is controlling, this is highly frustrating.

Obviously, in business, there are many times you want to have a meeting of the minds, or you need others to see things as you do. You have to sell yourself and your ideas to those you work with. In certain instances, you must exert your opinions, influence, even power to get something done. There are times you must insist on getting your way or think of clever and creative ways to get others to think differently. That's all part of business. And that's absolutely not what I'm referring to here. We're not talking about healthy, nor-mal attempts to come to a meeting of the minds or balancing points of view. We're also not talking about not caring about the behavior of others—of course you care. Rather, we're discussing the ways that insistence, singular thinking, rigidity, and the need to control trans-lates into pain and stress.

What hurts the controlling person is what goes on inside—his feelings and emotions. The key element seems to be a lack of willing-ness to allow other people to fully be themselves, to give them space to be who they are, and to respect—really respect—the fact that peo-ple think differently. Deep down, a controlling person doesn't want other people to be themselves, but rather the image of who they want them to be. But people aren't an image of who we want them to be—they are who they are. So, if you're tied to an imagined image, you're going to feel frustrated and impotent a great deal of the time. A con-trolling person assumes that he knows what's best, and by golly, he's going to make other people see the folly of their ways. Within the need to control, there's an inherent lack of respect for the opinions and ways of others.

The only way to become less controlling is to see the advantages of doing so. You have to see that you can still get your way when it's necessary, yet you will be less personally invested. In other words, less will be riding on other people being, thinking, or behaving in a certain way. This will translate into a far less stressful way of being in the world. When you can make allowances in your mind for the fact that other people see life differently than you do, you'll experience far less internal struggle.

In addition, as you become less controlling, you'll be a lot easier to be around. You can probably guess that most people don't like to be controlled. It's a turnoff. It creates resentment and adversarial relationships. As you let go of your need to be so controlling, people will be more inclined to help you; they will want to see you succeed. When people feel accepted for who they are rather than judged for who you think they should be, they will admire and respect you like never before.

29

Don't Dramatize the Deadlines

Many of us work under the constant demands of tight deadlines. Authors are no exception to this rule. But have you ever stopped to think about how much mental and emotional emphasis we put on our deadlines? And have you ever wondered what negative consequences are attached to such emphasis? If not, I encourage you to give these questions some careful consideration.

It's true that deadlines are a fact of life. Yet a lot of this type of stress comes not so much from the deadline itself, but from all the thinking about it, wondering whether or not we will make it, feeling sorry for ourselves, complaining, and, perhaps most of all, commiserating with others.

Recently, I was in an office waiting for an appointment. The person I was to meet with had been delayed in traffic. I was trying to read, but became fascinated by a conversation between two co-workers in the office. They were complaining among themselves about the unfair tight deadline they were on. Apparently, they had less than two hours to complete some type of report. Whatever it was, it was to be turned in by noon that same day.

I sat there, listening in amazement, as the two of them spent almost an entire hour complaining about how ridiculous it was to be put through this. They had not taken the first step toward the completion of their goal! Finally, about a minute before the person I was to meet finally arrived, one of them said in a frantic tone, "God, we'd better get started. It's due in an hour."

I realize that this is an extreme example, and few of us would waste time in as dramatic a manner as this. However, it does illustrate the point that the deadline itself isn't always the sole factor in the creation of stress. Ultimately, these two people seemed to realize that they could get the job done—even in one hour. So you have to wonder how different their experience could have been had they calmly taken a deep breath and worked together as quickly and efficiently as possible.

It's been my experience that complaining about deadlines—even if the complaints are justified—takes an enormous amount of mental energy and, more important to deadlines, time! The turmoil you go through commiserating with others or simply within your own head is rarely worth it. The added obsessive thinking about the deadline creates its own internal anxiety.

I know that deadlines can create quite a bit of stress and that sometimes it doesn't seem fair. However, working toward your goal without the interference of negative mental energy makes any job more manageable. See if you can notice how often you tend to worry, fret, or complain about deadlines. Then, try to catch yourself in the act of doing so. When you do, gently remind yourself that your energy would be better spent elsewhere. Who knows, perhaps you can ultimately make peace with deadlines altogether.

30

Remember the Phrase,
"Being Dead Is Bad for Business"

Several years ago my father was involved in a wonderful organization called BENZ, which stands for Business Executives for National Security. One of their missions was to educate business professionals about the absurdity of the nuclear arms race, both the financial burdens as well as the outright dangers to all of us. One of my favorite sayings that came out of BENZ was, "Being dead is bad for business." In a humorous way, they were emphasizing the obvious—if we blow ourselves up, none of us will prosper!

I'll bet you can guess where I'm going with this one. You can, of course, easily extend this clever metaphor to the way we treat ourselves—particularly in the areas of our personal health. The saying holds true however you look at it: Being dead is bad for business.

Remembering this really helps to keep things in perspective. For example, when you find yourself saying things like, "I don't have time to exercise," what you really should be saying is, "I don't have time *not* to exercise." If you lose your health and sense of well-being, you won't make it to work at all. In the long run, it takes far less time to take care of yourself than it does to lose your ability to function well.

Jim was a partner for a large New York law firm. Although he loved his family as much as anyone I've ever met, he was burning the candle at both ends. He left early and came home late. He traveled a great deal and was under constant stress. His children were growing up and he was missing most of it. He lacked sleep and exercise. He said to me, "Richard, this pace is going to kill me." To make matters worse, there didn't seem to be any light at the end of the tunnel. The more valuable he became to the firm, the more demands were made of his time.

At some point, it all became too much. After a great deal of personal reflection, he came to the conclusion that, as important as his work was to him, it wasn't worth dying for, nor was it worth missing the opportunity to watch his own children grow up. He decided a change was in order. He quit the firm and opened his own practice. I've never seen a more magnificent transformation. Not too long ago, he said to me, "I've never been happier. Business is better than ever and, for the first time, I'm able to spend a considerable amount of time with Julie and the kids." Although he still works very hard, he has created a sense of balance that works well for him. There's little question that, had he continued on his earlier path, his health and happiness would have continued to deteriorate. It seems that he literally decided that being dead would be bad for business!

Obviously, not everyone can make such a dramatic and risky change, but doesn't it make sense to eat well, exercise, get plenty of rest, think positively, have regular physical checkups, and partake in other healthy habits? In addition to the obvious problems associated with ignoring these commonsense health habits, you can see that it's also a horrible waste of time in the long run. Each cold or flu costs you days of productive work time. Who knows how many years of time you will save by simply taking care of yourself?

By remembering that "being dead is bad for business," you'll probably begin taking better care of yourself—physically and emotionally. You'll feel better, be happier, and probably live longer. You can let go of your fear that you'll fall behind because, in fact, you'll be more productive and have a longer, happier career. So keep yourself alive and healthy. It's good for business.

31

Don't Sweat the Demanding Boss

I'd estimate that a large percentage of adults that I know are either working for, or have worked for, a demanding boss. Like deadlines, taxes, and budgets, demanding bosses seem to be a fact of life for many working people. Even if you don't technically work "for" someone else, you may have demanding people that you work with or who pay your bills, or demanding customers you must attempt to please.

Like everything else, there are two ways to deal with demanding bosses. We can, like most do, complain about them, talk behind their backs, wish they would go away, secretly plot against them in our minds, wish them ill will, and feel forever stressed about the situation. Or we can take a different path and try (hard as it is) to stay focused on the positive aspects of the demanding party.

This was a particularly difficult concept for me to embrace, as I've always hated it when I feel pushed to perform. However, after dealing with many, many pushy people in my career, I've come to realize some important things.

The first "saving grace" I realized about demanding people is that, generally speaking, they are demanding to everyone. In other words, it's not personal. Before I recognized this to be the case, I would assume, as many do, that Mr. or Mrs. Demanding was "out to get me." I took their demanding demeanor personally and felt pressured. I would then compound the problem by thinking about his or her hidden motives, making a case within my own head as to why I had "a right to be angry." I would even go home at night and complain to poor Kris, who had already heard my story many times before.

All this began to change as I began to see a hint of innocence in the demanding party. In other words, I began to see that, in a very real sense, he or she really couldn't help it—they were stuck in the role of being demanding. This didn't change my preference for working with less-demanding people, but it did make it easier to accept when I had to.

I was working on a book a number of years ago when I was forced to work with a very demanding editor. I was having a difficult time with all the criticism and pushing, when a friend of mine asked me a very important question. She said, "Has it ever occurred to you that the most demanding people are often the ones who push you out of your comfort zone and help you rise to a new level of competence?" Until that moment, it hadn't occurred to me that this was true. As I look back at my career, I now realize that it was often the case that demanding people were the ones who brought out the best in me. Everything—from my writing style, to my ability to use a computer and adjust to technology, to my ability to speak in public—was greatly enhanced by my connection to demanding, even abrasive people.

Suzanne worked for someone who could only be described as "a real jerk." She described him as "a person who was demanding for no other reason than to be demanding." He seemed to feel a perverse sense of power when he was ordering people around.

Other than Suzanne, everyone in the office was either frightened or resentful of this demanding boss. For some reason, she had the wisdom to see through his huge ego and obnoxious behavior. Whenever possible, she tried to see the humor in her situation and instead of hating him, to see if there were things she might learn from his skills rather than focusing on his flaws. Her learning curve was sharp. It wasn't too long before her ability to stay cool in a hostile environment was noticed by her boss's employer, and she was promoted to a more interesting position in a different department.

The realization that there are two sides to demanding people—positive and negative—has made my entire life, especially my work life, a whole lot easier. Whereas before I would become defensive and dread the process, I now approach demanding people in an entirely new way. I'm open to what they may have to teach me, and I don't take their behavior personally. What has happened is quite remarkable. Because I'm so much less adversarial and defensive than I used to be, the "demanding" people I meet and work with seem to be a lot easier to be around. I now realize that my overreaction to demanding people had a lot to do with how difficult they were for me to deal with. As is so often the case, as I have grown and have been willing to open my mind to my own contribution to my problems, I have been rewarded with an easier life. I'm not advocating demanding behavior, as I still see it as a negative and abrasive personality trait. However, I have learned to take it in stride and see it as "small stuff." Perhaps the same can happen to you.

32

Don't Take the 20/80 Rule Personally

According to the 20/80 "rule," it's allegedly the case that in the work-place, 20 percent of the people do approximately 80 percent of the work. When I'm in a cynical mood, it sometimes seems that this ratio is grossly understated!

It's often the case that people who are highly productive or who have an intense work ethic don't understand why everyone else isn't just like them. It can be frustrating for these people to observe, work with, or in some cases, even be in the presence of people whom they perceive to be less productive than they should be—people who appear to get less done than they could. For some reason, they take it personally and allow it to bother them.

I've observed that many "overachievers" don't even see themselves as achievers—but rather as ordinary people who simply do what it takes to succeed or get the job done. They honestly don't understand why everyone isn't just like them. I once knew a super-achieving man who insisted, "I'm not an overachiever. It's just that most people are underachievers." I knew him well enough to know that he wasn't intentionally being arrogant. Rather, he was sharing with me the way he really saw the world. He honestly felt that most people don't work hard enough and almost no one lives up to their full potential. If you really believed this to be true, you can imagine how frustrated and irritated you would be most of the time. You'd be programmed to see everything that wasn't getting done, or that could or should be done differently. You would see the world in terms of its deficiencies.

You may not have such an extreme vision (I certainly don't), but you too may see the world from highly productive, efficient eyes. If so, it may be hard to accept (or understand) that other people have different priorities, work ethics, comfort levels, gifts, abilities, and mind-sets. People see things from entirely different perspectives and work at vastly different speeds. Remember, different people also define productivity in very different ways.

An easy way to come to peace with this productivity issue is to pay less attention to what other people *aren't* doing, and put more emphasis on what you get out of your own level of productivity—financially, energetically, emotionally, even spiritually. In other words, it's helpful to admit that you prefer to be a highly productive individual—it's your choice. And along with this choice come certain benefits. You may feel better about yourself than if you were less productive, or feel that you are fulfilling your mission or living up to your potential. Perhaps you make more money, or enjoy your work more than you would if you were less productive. You may have a more financially secure future, or an increased likelihood of opening certain doors for yourself. Or you may alleviate anxiety by getting a certain amount of work done each day. In other words, you have a number of payoffs that are driving you. Therefore, you are not a victim of those people who make different choices, or who, for whatever reason, aren't as productive as you, at least according to your standards.

To put this issue into perspective, it's helpful to think about your own work ethic, preferred pace of work, and overall ability to get things done. Ask yourself these questions: "Do I base my productivity choices on what others think I should be doing?" "Am I attempting to frustrate and irritate others by the pace of my work?" Of course not. Your choices are the result of your own rhythm, preferred pace of work, and desired results. Although you may be required to perform at a certain level, your overall productivity level stems from your own decisions and perceived payoffs.

The same is true for everyone else. It's not personal—it's not about you or me. Each person decides from within him or herself how much work is appropriate, all things considered. Everyone must weigh the pros and cons, consider the tradeoffs, and decide how hard they are going to work—and how productive they are going to be.

You may depend on other people—colleagues, coworkers, subcontractors, employees—to adhere to certain standards and levels of productivity. I certainly do. I'm not suggesting that you ease up or that you lower your standards. Instead, I'm suggesting that there's a way to look at varying levels of productivity in a healthy and productive way that can keep you from getting so upset and from taking it personally. I've found that when I'm able to maintain my perspective, and keep my own stress level under control, it's easy for me to bring out the absolute best in people without making them feel defensive or resentful.

I encourage you to examine your own subtle demands and expectations that others work the way you do. Once you accept the fact that it's not personal, you'll probably be able to lighten up enough to appreciate the differences in people and the way they choose to work. If so, you're going to feel more peaceful and relaxed.

33

Make Friends with Your Receptionist

Not too long ago I was in San Francisco in a reception lounge, waiting for my lunch partner. I was lucky enough to be a witness to the following chain of events which were so to the point of this book, I immediately knew I would like to share them with you.

A man walked in and barked out, in an unfriendly and demanding tone, "Any messages?" The female receptionist looked up and smiled. In a pleasant tone she answered, "No, sir." He responded in a nasty, almost threatening manner, "Just be sure to call me when my twelve-thirty appointment arrives. Got it?" He stormed down the hall.

No more than a minute later, a woman entered the room who apparently also wanted to know if she had any messages. She smiled, said "hello," and asked the receptionist if she was having a nice day. The receptionist smiled back and thanked the woman for asking. She then proceeded to hand the woman a stack of messages and shared with her some additional information which I could not hear. They laughed together a few times before the woman thanked the receptionist and walked down the hall.

It's always shocked me when I've seen someone who isn't friendly to the receptionist or who takes him or her for granted. It seems like such an obviously short-sighted business decision. Over the years

I've asked many receptionists whether or not they treat everyone in the office equally. Most of the time I receive a response such as, "You're kidding, right?" Indeed, it seems that receptionists have a great deal of power—and being friendly to them can make your life a lot easier. Not only does being nice to your receptionist all but ensure a friendly hello and someone to trade smiles with a few times a day, but in addition, your receptionist can do a great many intangible things for you—protect your privacy and screen calls, remind you of important events, alert you to potential problems, help you prioritize and pace yourself, and on and on.

I've seen both ends of the spectrum. I've seen receptionists protect people they work with from a variety of unnecessary hassles, even save them from major mistakes. I once saw a receptionist run down the hall and all the way down the street to remind someone of a meeting she was sure the person was going to forget. I later asked the person who was chased to tell me what had happened. He verified that the receptionist had been his "hero." He went so far as to claim that she may have even saved his job. When I asked this receptionist about their rapport, she informed me that they weren't really friends, but that he was an extremely nice person. I asked her if that had anything to do with her willingness to run down the street in the hot sun to remind him of a meeting. She just smiled and said, "You get right to the point, don't you?"

Sadly, the opposite can occur when a receptionist feels taken for granted or resentful of someone. I've heard stories of receptionists who have mysteriously "lost" messages, or who have failed to remind someone of a meeting, because it was inconvenient to do so.

Obviously, there are plenty of great receptionists who are able to set aside their personal feelings and do what is best, most if not all of the time. But think about this issue from the perspective of the receptionist. He or she might answer the phone, respond to the messages for a relatively large number of people, and have a number of other important responsibilities. Some of the people they work with are really nice, most are moderately so, and a few are jerks. Isn't it obvious that being friendly to your receptionist is in your best interest? Aside from the fact that it's their job, what possible motivation does a receptionist have to go the extra mile, or do something they aren't officially being paid to do, if you aren't nice to them—or at very least respectful?

In no way am I suggesting that you make friends with your receptionist just to get something in return. Primarily, you want to do so simply because it's a nice thing to do and because it will brighten the workday for both of you. After all, your receptionist is someone you see on a daily basis. But aside from that, it's just good business and it takes so little time or effort. My suggestion is to think of your receptionist as a key partner in your life. Treat them as if you truly value them—as you should. Be kind, genuine, patient, and courteous. Thank them when they do something for you—even if it's part of their job. Can you imagine the stress and other possible consequences of missing just one of those important phone calls—or a single important message? It's your receptionist who prevents that from happening. Wouldn't it seem wise to include your receptionist on your holiday shopping list? Incidentally, the same principle applies to many other roles as well, in different ways—the janitor, housecleaner, managers, cook, and so on.

I think you'll find that making friends with your receptionist is a wise thing to do. It's a great way to brighten your day-to-day work life, as well as an effective way to make your life a little less stressful. If you haven't already done so, I encourage you to give it a try.

Be Careful What You Ask For

Many of us spend a great deal of time wishing things were different. We dream of a "better job," more responsibility, less of this, and more of that. Sometimes, the things we spend our energy longing for actually do (or would) improve the quality of our life. Other times, however, the very things we wish for are hardly worth the tradeoffs, or the effort. For this reason, I suggest you be really careful what you ask for.

The purpose of this strategy isn't to encourage you to stop dreaming of, or working toward, a better life, but to remind you that sometimes your life is pretty darn good exactly the way it is. My goal here is to remind you to carefully think through what it is you think you want, because you just might end up getting it, which is often more than you bargained for—more frustration, more grief, more travel, more responsibility, more conflict, more demands on your time, and so forth. When you think in these terms, it often helps you reconnect with your gratitude and realize that perhaps things aren't as bad as we sometimes make them out to be.

I've met plenty of people who spent years focused on how much better their lives were going to be when certain things occurred—i.e., when they were finally promoted to various positions—so much so that they took for granted the good parts of the position they already had. In other words, they were so focused on what was wrong with their careers that they failed to enjoy and appreciate the gifts they were enjoying all along.

For example, a man I knew dreamed of a job he felt would be "so much better" within the same company he was working with. He lobbied for that job for quite some time, constantly complaining about his current position. It wasn't until he finally secured that job that he realized the major tradeoffs that were involved. It was true that he had a bit more prestige and a slightly better salary, yet he was now forced to travel several days a week, often much more often than that. He missed his three kids terribly and started missing important events—soccer games, music performances, teacher conferences, and other special dates. In addition, his relationship with his wife became strained as their relatively peaceful routine was set aside for the alleged "better life." He was also forced to scale way back on his much-loved exercise routine due to his busier, less flexible schedule.

A woman I knew worked hard to convince her boss that she deserved to telecommute instead of coming into the office. She succeeded. The problem was, she never realized (until a month later) that, despite the dreaded traffic, she actually loved coming into the city each day. This was her chance to be with friends at lunch and after work. It was her social structure, her chance to be with people. She also missed lunches at local cafes, her favorite music that she listened to on her way to work, and other taken-for-granted simple pleasures. After a while, she began to feel trapped in her own home.

Other people crave power or fame. Only after they achieve it do they realize that the lack of any real privacy is a real drag. Instead of anonymity, which most of us take for granted, people are now looking over their shoulders. They are often exposed to more criticism and closer scrutiny.

I want to emphasize that I'm not taking a negative stance on any of these tradeoffs. Often, making more money is crucial, and outweighs any other consideration you might have. For many people, traffic is almost unbearable and would be worth avoiding at almost any price. Some people love the spotlight and the increased visibility. The important point here isn't the specifics, or any sort of value judgment, but the recognition of the relevance of asking yourself the important questions—"What am I really asking for, and why?"

When thinking about your job or career, it's important to consider what's right and good about your work in addition to focusing on what might be better. Feeling satisfied or being happy doesn't mean you aren't still working hard to make your career as successful as possible. You can have both—happiness and drive—without sacrificing your sanity.

Keep in mind that more responsibility might be a great thing, but it could very well lead to less personal freedom, privacy, and so forth. Similarly, a better paying position might make you feel more financially secure and it might be worth it—but you may give up other things that you haven't yet considered, or that you simply take for granted. It's all just food for thought. Remember, be careful what you ask for, because you might just get it—and more.

35

Absorb the Speed Bumps of Your Day

A metaphor I've found helpful in my own life is that of a speed bump. Rather than labeling the issues that come up during a typical work day as problems, I think of them as speed bumps. An actual speed bump, as you know, is a low bump in a road designed to get your attention and slow you down. Depending on how you approach and deal with the bump, it can be a miserable, uncomfortable, even damaging experience, or it can simply be a temporary slow down—no big deal.

If you step on the gas, speed up, and tighten the wheel, for example, you'll hit the bump with a loud thump! Your car may be damaged, you'll make a great deal of noise, and you can even injure yourself. In addition, you'll add unnecessary wear and tear to your car, and you'll look foolish and obnoxious to other people. If, however, you approach the bump softly and wisely, you'll be over it in no time. You'll suffer no adverse effects, and your car will be completely unaffected. Let's face it. Either way, you're likely to get over the bump. How you (and your car) feel once you get over it, however, is an entirely different issue.

If you ski or ride bikes, you already know how this works. If you tighten up your body, it's difficult to absorb the bump. Your form will be terrible and you may even fall. The bump will seem bigger than it really is.

Problems can be looked at in a similar light. You can be annoyed by them, think about how unfair and awful they are, complain about them and commiserate with others. You can remind yourself, over and over again, how difficult life is and how this problem is yet another justification for why you "have a right" to be upset! You can tighten up. Unfortunately, this is the way many people approach their problems.

When you think of your problems as speed bumps, however, they begin to look very different. You'll begin to expect a number of speed bumps to present themselves during a typical day. Like riding a bike, bumps are simply a part of the experience. You can fight and resist, or you can relax and accept. As a problem shows up during your day, you can begin to say to yourself, "Ah, here's another one." Then, like the ski mogul or bump on your bike ride, you begin to relax into it, thereby absorbing the shock, making it seem less significant. Then you can calmly decide what action or decision is likely to get you over this hurdle in the most effective, graceful manner. Like skiing, the calmer and more relaxed you remain, the easier it is to maneuver.

Thinking of problems as speed bumps encourages you to say things like, "I wonder what the best way to get through this one might be?" There is a healthy element of detachment involved, where you're looking at the problem objectively rather than reactively, looking for the path of least resistance. In other words, you assume there is an answer; you just need to find out what it is. This is in sharp contrast to seeing such concerns as problems, where it's tempting to think in terms of emergencies.

If you think about your work life, you'll probably agree that in one way or another, you do manage to get through a vast majority of the problems you are confronted with. If you didn't, you probably wouldn't last long in whatever it is you are doing. That being the case, where is the logic in panicking and in treating each problem like a major disaster?

My guess is that if you experiment with this one—simply thinking and labeling your problems as speed bumps instead of problems—you're going to be pleasantly surprised at how much more manageable your day is going to seem. After all, problems can be really tough, but almost anyone can maneuver over a speed bump.

36

Never, Ever Backstab

I was attending a corporate function prior to being a guest speaker when a young man approached me and introduced himself. He seemed nice enough until he launched into his backstabbing mode.

He moaned and complained about his boss and many other people he worked with. Within ten minutes, I became an expert on the "dirt" in his company. If I were to believe his version of the story, his entire firm was completely screwed up—except, of course, for himself.

The sad part of it was that I don't even think he was aware that he was doing it—it seemed to be a part of his ordinary conversation. Apparently, backstabbing was something that he was in the habit of doing.

Unfortunately, this man is not alone in this tendency. As someone who travels to diverse groups of people in different parts of the country, I'm sorry to report that backstabbing is alive and well. Perhaps one of the reasons it's so prevalent is that too few of us consider the consequences.

There are two very good reasons never again to backstab. First of all, it sounds terrible and makes you look really bad. When I hear someone slamming someone behind his back, it says nothing about the person they are referring to, but it does say a great deal about their own need to be judgmental. To me, someone who slams a person behind his back is disingenuous or two-faced. I doubt very much that the man I'm referring to in the above example said the things to his coworkers that he said to me. In other words, he would put on a smile and say nice things to them but, behind their backs, he would act in a completely different way. To me that's not fair play, and it's a poor reflection on oneself.

But aside from being a mean-spirited and unfair thing to do that makes you look bad, it's important to realize that backstabbing creates other problems for you as well. It causes stress, anxiety, and other negative feelings.

The next time you hear someone backstabbing someone else, try to imagine how the offending person actually feels—beneath the confident, secure appearance. How does it feel to say nasty, offensive, and negative things about someone else who isn't even there to defend themselves? Obviously, that's a loaded question—but the answer is so obvious that it's almost embarrassing to discuss. I know that when I have backstabbed in the past, my words have left me with an uncomfortable feeling. I remember asking myself the question, "How could you stoop so low?" You simply can't win. You may get a moment or two of relief from getting something off your chest, but you have to live with your words for the rest of the day— and longer.

Backstabbing also causes anxiety. The man I was talking to was sure to speak in a quiet voice—he didn't want to be heard. Wouldn't it be easier and less stressful to speak kindly about others, in a respectful tone? When you do, you don't have to worry whether or not someone will overhear your conversation or share your backstabbing stories with others—perhaps with the person you're attacking behind his back. Indeed, when you backstab, the pressure's on—you're on guard, now forced to protect your secret. It's not worth the price!

Finally, it's absolutely predictable that if you backstab someone, you will lose the respect and trust of the people you are sharing with. Remember, most of the people you're sharing with are your friends or colleagues. It's important to realize that, even if they appear to enjoy what you are saying, and even if they too are participating in the gossip, there will always be a part of them that knows that you are capable of backstabbing. They've seen it firsthand. It's inevitable that they will ask themselves the question, "If he will talk behind someone else's back, wouldn't he be capable of doing the same thing to me?" What's more, they know that the answer is yes.

One of the nicest compliments I ever received was when someone with whom I have a great deal of contact said to me, "I've never heard you say a mean thing about anyone." Unfortunately, as I mentioned above, I have said mean things about others behind their backs, and I'm not proud of it. However, I took this compliment to heart because I'm doing my best to avoid backstabbing at all costs.

No one bats 100 percent. An occasional comment or the sharing of feelings probably isn't going to cause you great stress or ruin your reputation. But, all things being equal, it's a really good idea to put backstabbing out to pasture, forever.

37

Lower Your Expectations

I was sharing this idea with a large group of people when someone in the back of the room raised his hand and said, "What kind of an optimist are you, suggesting that we lower our expectations?" His question was a valid one and, in fact, you might be wondering the same thing.

It's a delicate question to answer because, on one hand, you absolutely want to have high expectations and to expect that things will work out well. You want to believe that success is inevitable, and that your experiences will generally be positive. And with hard work and some really good luck, many (perhaps even most) of these expectations may indeed come true.

On the other hand, when you expect too much from life, when you are unrealisitc and demanding, you set yourself up for disappointment and a great deal of unnecessary grief. You'll probably also alienate at least some of the people you work with, because most people don't appreciate being held to unrealistic expectations. Your expectation is that the events in your life will evolve in a certain predictable way, and that people will behave according to your plans. When they don't, which is often the case, you end up stressed-out and miserable.

Often simply lowering your expectations, even slightly, can make your day (and your life) seem a whole lot easier. You can create an emotional environment for yourself whereby, when things do work out well, rather than taking them for granted, you'll be pleasantly surprised and grateful. And when your expectations don't go according to plan, it won't devastate you. Lowering your expectations helps to keep you from being so surprised when you bump into hassles and "stuff" to deal with. Instead of reacting negatively, you'll be able to say, "Oh well, I'll take care of it." Keeping your composure allows you to deal with the irritant or solve the problem, and be done with it.

Life just isn't neat and trouble-free. People make mistakes, and we all have bad days. Sometimes people are rude or insensitive. No job is entirely secure, and no matter how much money you make, it probably doesn't seem like enough. Phone lines and computers occasionally break down, along with everything else.

When I met Melissa, she worked for a software development company. She described it as her first "real job." She was young and driven, and had exceptionally high expectations. The problem was, many of her expectations weren't being met. She wasn't being treated with the degree of respect she wanted (or expected), and her ideas weren't being taken seriously. She felt under-appreciated and taken for granted. She was frustrated and burned-out.

I suggested she lower her expectations and consider thinking of her job in a new way. Rather than expecting her job to be all things to her, I asked if she might see it as a stepping stone to bigger and better things later on. She took the suggestion to heart, and her world began to change for the better. Without the mental distraction regarding what needs *weren't* being met, she was able to focus on the most essential aspects of her work. Her learning curve accelerated, and her stress level dropped.

About a year later, I received a nice voice mail message from Melissa letting me know how helpful it had been to lower her expectations. Specifically she said, "I don't know why I made such a big deal about everything. Obviously, every job has tradeoffs to deal with. I guess I've learned to have a little more perspective and to take things in stride." She must have been doing something right, as she has been promoted twice since the last time I spoke to her.

Many people confuse expectations with standards of excellence. Please understand that I'm not suggesting that you lower your standards or accept poor performance as okay. Nor am I saying you shouldn't hold people accountable. What I'm referring to is making room in your heart for bad moods, mistakes, errors, and glitches. Instead of spending so much time being annoyed about the way things unfold, you will be able to take most of it in stride. Life and its many challenges won't get to you as much. This will conserve your energy and, ultimately, make you more productive.

Make no mistake: You'll still want to do everything possible to put the odds in your favor—work hard, plan ahead, do your part, be creative, prepare well, solicit the help of others, be a team player. However, no matter how hard you try, life still isn't always going to go as planned. One of the best ways to deal with this inevitability is to stop expecting it to be otherwise. So ease off your expectations a little, and see how much nicer your life can be. You won't be disappointed.

38

Stop Wishing You Were Somewhere Else

If you reflect on the insidious tendency to be wishing you were somewhere else, you may agree that it's a silly, even self-destructive thing to do. Before you jump up and say, "Wait a minute, I don't do that," let me explain what I mean.

There are many ways that we spend time wishing we were somewhere else. We'll be at work and wish we were home. Or during the middle of the week we might be wishing it were Friday. Sometimes we wish we were doing something else with our careers. We wish we had different responsibilities or could spend our time with different people. We wish our boss were different, or our employees. We wish our working environment were different or that we had a different kind of commute. We wish our industry were different, or that our competition would respond differently, or that our circumstances would change. This list could obviously go on. The problem is, these wishes aren't reality, but rather, they are thoughts of a different reality.

If you're not careful, you can begin to wish your life away, always wishing you were somewhere other than where you actually are. But you're not somewhere else. Rather, you're right here. This is reality. One of my favorite quotes is, "Life is what's happening while we're busy making other plans." A slightly different version might be,

"Life is what's happening while we're wishing we were somewhere else." When you are wishing you were somewhere else, it's almost as though you are one step removed from life rather than actually being in it, open to life exactly as it is.

From a practical standpoint, it's very difficult to be focused and effective when your mind is preoccupied with where it would rather be. In fact, the two are a contradiction in terms. Your concentration suffers because there is a lack of engagement, a lack of zeroing in on what's truly significant. In addition, it's virtually impossible to enjoy yourself and what you are doing when you're focused more on where you'd rather be than where you actually are. Think about the things you enjoy most. In all cases, they are activities where you are completely absorbed in the moment, really focused on what you're doing. In the absence of the focus, the joy you experience is diminished. How much fun is it to read a good novel when you're thinking about something else?

But here's where this bit of wisdom gets a little tricky. When you're not getting any pleasure out of your work, it's easy to say, "Of course I'd rather be somewhere else, I'm not enjoying myself." But step back for a moment and take a closer look at what's contributing to the lack of enjoyment. The question is what comes first—a lack of enjoyment, or a mind that is focused elsewhere? Not all but at least some of the time, the boredom or lack of satisfaction we feel is caused not by our careers or by how we are spending our time, but by the lack of focus in our thinking. The fact that you're thinking about where you'd rather be is literally sapping the joy out of what you're doing.

I think you'll be pleasantly surprised, even shocked, if you make the decision to spend less time wishing you were somewhere else and more time focused on what you're actually doing. You may regain your spark and enthusiasm for your work, and in doing so, begin to have more fun. Plus, because you'll be more focused, you'll be more creative and productive as well.

Obviously, I'm not suggesting that it's not appropriate or important to plan for the future or dream. Nor am I saying you shouldn't make changes when you are drawn to do so. These are wonderful things to do and are very often appropriate. However, when you become more immersed in what you are doing instead of what you'd rather be doing, both the nature of your dreams as well as your planned course of action will begin to change. If you have a dream, the path to get there will become clear and obvious. Instead of being distracted by your conflicting and worried thoughts, you'll have a clear mind loaded with wisdom. Good luck on this one. I think you're going to find yourself enjoying your work more than you ever thought possible.

39

Give Up Your Fear of Speaking to Groups

I used to be absolutely petrified of speaking in front of any type of group. In fact, I was so scared that I actually fainted (twice) in high school while attempting to do so.

But I'm not alone. I've heard that public speaking is the number one fear in America. It seems that speaking to groups is even more frightening to people than air travel, bankruptcy, even death!

Just for fun, I ran this strategy by a respected friend of mine to see whether or not he understood why I would include this specific strategy in a book on becoming less stressed at work. His specific response was, "I know that speaking in public is a huge fear, but how would becoming less frightened to do so help you sweat the small stuff less at work?"

It's a fair question, but I have the answer.

A fear as big as this one doesn't exist in a vacuum. In other words, it doesn't show up only on those occasions when you are called on to speak in front of a group. Instead, the stress associated with speaking in front of others looms over you, perhaps very subtly, if there is any chance whatsoever that you will ever need to speak in front of people. Whether you may be required to give a presentation, a sales pitch, the results of a report or study, an all-out speech, or simply share an idea with others, the stress factor is the same—enormous—if you're scared.

Another factor to consider is this: If you're frightened of speaking to groups, even a little bit, you may avoid doing things that could greatly benefit your career, give you a promotion or more responsibility, or an advancement of some kind. Before I overcame my fear of speaking, I remember making many decisions based on the likelihood that I may or may not have to speak. Getting over this fear helped me to relax about my work so that I could focus on other things. It made my work life easier and far less stressful. There is no question that overcoming this fear has also helped me to become more successful as an author. Had I not done so, I doubt very much that I would be writing books, because writing books requires promoting them, often in front of huge groups of people.

If you have any fear whatsoever, I urge you to consider this suggestion very carefully. Once you get over the fear you experience, you will be less stressed and more easygoing in your work life. This will help you be more creative and solution-oriented because the distraction of this fear will be gone forever. Because you'll be less on edge, you'll be sweating the small stuff less and less.

The way to get over this fear is to put yourself in situations where you are required to speak to groups. You can start really small—even one or two others is a great place to start. There are classes you can take, coaches who can help you, books to read, and tapes to listen to. There are a variety of methods and strategies to look into. In the end, however, you'll have to take the first step and get in front of people. If you do, I think you'll find, as I have, that if you get over this common fear, you'll be richly rewarded in terms of the quality of your work and, indeed, the quality of your life.

40

Avoid the Tendency to Put a Cost on Personal Things

One of the stressful habits that many of us get into at work is that we tend to put a cost on too many things. In other words, we calculate in our minds the cost of what we are doing or owning—when we could be doing or owning something else. Obviously, there are times when this is enormously helpful, such as when we spend time watching television or organizing our desk when we could be spending that same time working on the report that is due tomorrow morning. In this case, it might be helpful to remind yourself that, in effect, that television program is carrying with it an enormous cost—perhaps even your job.

I remember when Kris and I bought a one-fifth interest in a sailboat. The only problem was that during the next two years we only stepped on that boat once—and even then it was for a picnic with our best friends, not for a sail. In this case, it was helpful for Kris and me to realize that our picnic had, in effect, cost us over two thousand dollars! Oh well, at least we had a lot of fun on the picnic.

There are other times, however, when it's important that we not put a price tag on what we are doing. I've known quite a number of people, for example, who rarely take days off to spend time relaxing or doing something just for fun because the "cost is too high." They make the mistake of calculating what they could be earning during the days, or even hours, they are away. Even on those rare occasions when they do get away, they find it difficult to relax because they are so preoccupied with what they could be doing instead, or with what they might be missing. They will say or think things like, "If I were seeing clients (or earning) at a rate of fifty dollars an hour, I could be making four hundred dollars today. I shouldn't be here." And while they are technically correct in their arithmetic, they are effectively eliminating any possibility for a calm, inwardly rich life—because in order to achieve a less-stressed life, you must value and prioritize your need for recreation, fun, quiet, and family at least some of the time. So, even if your earning capacity is much less than the above example, there still has to be some limit on how out-of-balance you allow yourself to become.

One of my fondest memories growing up was one day that my dad helped me move from one apartment to another. It was during the week, and my dad simply took the day off. Looking back, it was a time when my father was busier than ever before. He was running a giant company and was dealing with some very complex issues. His time was extremely in demand and valuable. I remember thinking I was being financially clever when I said to him, "Dad, this is probably the costliest move ever made," referring to the fact that he could have easily hired a few people to help me at a tiny fraction of the actual cost of his being there with me. Doing so would have been far less stressful, much cheaper, and a lot easier on his back. Without even thinking about it he looked at me and said, "Rich, you can't put a price tag on spending time with your son. There's nothing in the world I'd rather be doing than spending time with you." Those words have stuck with me for almost twenty years, and will do so for the rest of my life. I probably don't have to tell you that my dad's comment meant more to me than all of the thousands of hours he spent in the office "for his family." It made me feel special, important, and valued. It also reminded him that his life was more than "another stressful day at the office."

If you want to reduce the stress in your life and be a happier person, I have found it to be useful to look at certain issues without attaching a price to them—spending time alone, with someone you love, or with your children. When you take time doing things that nourish you, or spending time with people you love, it reduces the stress you feel in all aspects of your life, including work. When you know that, no matter what, certain parts of your life simply aren't for sale—at any price—it reminds you that your life is precious and, furthermore, it belongs to you.

Go ahead and allow yourself to do some things just for you. Take some time for yourself—take a regular walk, visit nature, read more books, learn to meditate, get a massage, listen to music, go camping, spend more time with your loved ones or alone—but do something. And when you do, don't spend your time thinking about how you could be more productive. My guess is that if you learn to value your personal life and your true priorities, you'll discover that life will seem easier than before. You'll be surprised by the number of good ideas that will pop into your mind when you allow yourself to have fun—without calculating the cost.

41

When You Solicit Advice, Consider Taking It

One of the most interesting interpersonal dynamics that I've been able to observe is the tendency that many people have to share something that is bothering them, yet completely ignore the advice they receive in response. The reason I find this so interesting is because, as I have listened to conversations over the years, I've been impressed over and over again by a great deal of the creative advice I have heard. So often, it would appear as though the advice being given would solve the problem at hand, easily and quickly. In fact, there have been plenty of times that I've heard ideas designed for other people that were completely dismissed by the person to whom it was intended—that I've taken as a means of improving my life!

Obviously, there are times when we share a concern simply because we want to vent or because we simply want someone to listen to us. But there are other times when we are genuinely confused about what to do and actively seek advice, such as when we say, "I wish I knew what to do," or "Do you have any ideas?" Yet when a friend, spouse, coworker, or someone else offers a suggestion, our immediate response is to tune it out, or in some way dismiss it.

I don't know exactly why so many of us tend to dismiss the advice we receive. Perhaps we are embarrassed that we need help or we hear things we don't want to hear. Maybe we are too proud to admit that a friend or family member knows something we don't. Sometimes the advice we receive requires effort or a change in lifestyle. There are probably many other factors as well.

I'm the first to admit that I do many things wrong. But one of the qualities I'm most proud of—and am certain has helped me a great deal in both my personal and professional life—is my ability to really listen to advice, and in many instances, take it. I'm absolutely willing to admit that I don't have all the answers I need to make my life as effective and peaceful as possible. Usually, however, someone else can offer a suggestion that can help me. Not only do I often benefit from the advice I receive, but the person offering it to me is thrilled that I'm actually willing to listen and even *take* the advice. People have suggested that I talk too much—and they were right. I've been told I needed to become a better listener—and I did. People have suggested that I take a certain course or try a certain diet, and I have. And it really helped. Over and over again, I've asked people to share with me any blind spots they see in my attitude or behavior. As long as I remain receptive and nondefensive, I can almost always learn something. And sometimes, one simple suggestion can make a world of difference.

The trick is to be willing to admit that other people can see things about us (or our circumstances) that we may be too close to or too personally involved with to see ourselves. So, while you probably won't want to accept all the advice that comes your way, you may want to become just a little more open to some of it. My guess is, if you do, your life is going to be a whole lot easier.

42

Make Allowances for Incompetence

Like so many things, incompetence seems to be represented by a bell-shaped curve. There is always going to be a small percentage of people who are near the top, most people will fall somewhere near the middle, and a few will lie toward the bottom. In most professions (other than those where only highly competent people are considered qualified), it's just the way life seems to pan out. A few people in each field will be really good, most will be sort of average, and there will always be a few that make you wonder how in the world they manage to make a living.

It's interesting, however, that so many people don't seem to understand this dynamic or, if they do, they certainly don't exhibit any compassion or common sense in their reaction to it. Despite the fact that incompetence is an obvious and unavoidable fact of life, it's as though people are surprised, take it personally, feel imposed upon, and react harshly to it. Many people complain about incompetence, are bothered by it, discuss its rampant trend with others, and spend valuable time and energy hoping and wishing it would go away. I've seen people so upset about obvious incompetence that I thought they might have a heart attack or a nervous breakdown. Instead of seeing it as a necessary evil, they get all worked up, often compound the problem with their harsh reaction, and bang their head against the wall in frustration. In the end, nothing was accomplished except that the frustrated person had an emotional meltdown and made himself look bad.

One of my favorite television shows is the comedy *Mad About You*. The brilliant comedian Lisa Kudrow plays the part of an almost unimaginably incompetent waitress in a cafe. I assumed her role was non-duplicable until recently when I was in a restaurant in Chicago. My waitress was so bad that, for a moment, I thought I was being "set up" with a hidden camera to see if I would sweat the small stuff. As far as I could tell, she managed to get every single order completely messed up. I ordered a vegetarian sandwich and ended up with rare roast beef. The customer next to me ordered a milk shake and ended up with a bottle of beer which was quickly spilled on his expensive looking shirt. It went on and on, each table seemingly worse than the next. After a while, it actually became amusing. When the check arrived, she had charged me for the roast beef, the other man's beer, and a T-shirt with the restaurant's logo!

Another story comes from someone I met who works in a real estate office. In addition to selling homes, she helps coordinate her clients with the various professionals who put the deal together—lenders, inspectors, and appraisers. She told me of an appraiser she had worked with (twice) who had also worked with many of her colleagues. This appraiser was, in her words, "beyond belief." His job was to appraise the market value of the home being sold to be sure the loan was a reasonable risk for the lender. Apparently, he was in the habit of appraising homes for up to twice their actual value. She was selling one home, for example, that was worth approximately $150,000 that he appraised for $300,000. The almost identical home next door sold for $150,000. She claimed that this was his standard operating procedure—he would toss out all rational and standard appraisal methods and rely on his "instinct." His incompetence must have worked out pretty well for the buyers—but imagine the risk the lenders were taking with home appraisals that had no relationship to reality.

The most unbelievable part of this story is that, allegedly, this appraiser has managed to stay in business for more than ten years! Despite a lengthy pattern of blatant incompetence, he continues to be hired by lenders who depend on his judgment to protect their loans.

In no way am I saying it's pleasant to deal with incompetence, but if you want to avoid feeling so irritated, it's important that you stop being so surprised and caught off guard by it. It's helpful to understand that some degree of incompetence is about as predictable as an occasional rainy day—even if you live in California, as I do. Sooner or later, it's bound to happen. So, instead of saying, "I can't believe my eyes," or something similar, keep in mind that it's bound to occur every once in a while—it's inevitable. This acceptance of the way things really are will probably allow you to say (or think) something like, "Of course it's going to be like this from time to time." You'll be able to keep your perspective and remember that, a vast majority of the time, it's not personally directed at you. Rather than focusing on the most dramatic and extreme examples to validate your belief in rampant incompetence, see if you can recognize and appreciate the fact that most people do really well, most of the time. With a little practice and patience, you'll cease being so upset over things you have very little control over.

I'm not suggesting that you should put up with or advocate incompetence, or that, if you're an employer, you shouldn't replace incompetent employees with harder-working, more qualified people. These are totally different issues. What I'm saying is that, regardless of who you are or what you do, you are going to run into (and have to deal with) at least some amount of incompetence in your work life. Why not learn to take it in stride, and not let it bother you so much?

By simply making allowances in your mind for something that is going to happen anyway, you'll be able to dramatically improve the quality of your life. I know that dealing with incompetence can be frustrating—especially when the stakes are high. I can virtually guarantee you, however, that losing your cool isn't going to help very much.

The next time you run into incompetence, even if it's flagrant, see if you can make the best of it, rectify the situation if possible, and then go on with your day. Let it go. Rather than turning the incompetence into front page news in your mind, see if you can turn it into just another minor story. If you do, you'll be free from yet another of life's sources of frustration.

Don't Get Stressed by the Predictable

In many industries there are certain standard procedures or problems that are, to a large degree, predictable. The first few times they happen, or if you're caught off guard, it's understandable that they can create some anxiety or stress. However, once you factor them into your awareness, and you can predict how events are typically played out, it's silly to be annoyed and upset. Yet I find that many people continue to feel bothered and stressed, even after they see how the game is played. They continue to get upset, angry, and complain about a pattern that is predictable. To me, this is self-induced stress in its purest form.

I've had several fairly relaxed friends who are, or who have been, flight attendants for major airlines. Although they themselves are usually the type of people who take life in stride, they have shared with me some interesting stories about colleagues who fall apart (luckily without the passengers being aware) over absolutely predictable parts of their job.

One woman gets completely stressed out every time her flight is delayed. She calls her husband to complain about her stressful job, and shares her frustration with her friends (who have already heard the story hundreds of times). Rather than saying to herself, "Of course there are going to be occasional delays," she tortures herself by reacting to the predictable.

Another flight attendant (this one a male) gets super angry whenever he runs into a rude or unappreciative passenger. He's obviously bright enough to understand that this is bound to happen every once in a while (or probably more often than that). Yet, every time it happens, he goes crazy and feels compelled to share his anger with others. All he does is stir up the other flight attendants by getting them focused on the few disrespectful people instead of the vast majority who are quite pleasant.

I met an accountant who gets annoyed every March and April because his hours are increased and he can't leave the office at 5:00. He jumps up and down and complains about how "unfair" it is, even though it's absolutely predictable. It would seem to me that virtually *all* accountants who prepare income tax returns for a living would be the busiest during tax season. What am I missing?

I met a police officer who took it personally when people would drive faster than the speed limit. He would get frustrated and dish out harsh lectures, apparently forgetting that it was his job to catch people speeding to create safer roads. Again, this is a predictable part of his work. I've spoken to a number of other police officers who simply take this part of their job in stride—because they know it's coming, it's predictable. Most of them say, "Sure, we have to issue a citation, but why in the world would I get stressed out over it?"

Before you say, "Those are silly examples," or "I'd never get upset over something like that," take a careful look at your own industry. It's always easier to see why someone else shouldn't be upset than it is to admit that you, too, can make a bigger deal out of something than is really necessary. I admit I've made this mistake myself on more than one occasion, and perhaps you have too. By seeing certain aspects of your profession as predictable, you can alleviate a great deal of frustration.

Although the specific details and hassles are different in each industry and while many of the predictable events don't appear to make much sense, I've seen a similar pattern in many fields. In some industries, for example, there are built-in delays. You'll be waiting on suppliers, orders, or someone or something else in order to do your job, so it will always *seem* like you're running late and in an enormous hurry. And while it's true you have to wait until the last minute to get everything you need, it's entirely predictable and consistent— you know it's going to happen. Therefore, if you can make the necessary allowances in your mind for the inevitable, you won't have to feel the pressure. Instead, you learn to take it in stride. This doesn't mean you don't care. Obviously, it's necessary and appropriate to do your best job and work as quickly and efficiently as possible. To be surprised and resentful that you're constantly waiting for others is foolish.

In other fields (perhaps most of them), there is always more work to be done than time to do it. If you look around, you'll notice that everyone is in the same boat—it's set up that way. Work is designed to land on your desk slightly quicker than you're able to complete it. If you examine this tendency, you'll notice that it's absolutely predictable. If you worked twice as fast as you currently do, nothing would change in the sense of getting it all done. As you work faster and more efficiently, you'll notice that magically more work will appear. Again, this doesn't mean your work isn't demanding or that you shouldn't work hard and do your absolute best. It just means that you don't have to lose sleep over the fact that it's never going to be completely done—because it isn't.

As you see these and other work-related tendencies in their proper "predictable" perspective, you can eliminate a great deal of stress. You can make allowances in your mind, attitude, and behavior for that which you know is going to happen anyway. You can breathe easier and, perhaps, learn to relax a little more. I hope this added perspective is as helpful to you as it has been to me.

Don't Live in an Imagined Future

If you want to be a happier, less-stressed person, there is no better place to start than with becoming aware of what I like to call "anticipatory thinking," or an imagined future. Essentially, this type of thinking involves imagining how much better your life will be when certain conditions are met—or how awful, stressful, or difficult something is going to be at some point down the road. Typical anticipatory thinking sounds something like this: "I can't wait to get that promotion, then I'll feel important." "My life will be so much better when my 401K is fully funded." "Life will be so much simpler when I can afford an assistant." "This job is only a stepping stone to a better life." "These next few years will be really tough, but after that I'll be cruising." You get so carried away by your own thoughts that you remove yourself from the actual present moments of your life, thereby postponing the act of living effectively and joyfully.

There are other, more short-term forms of this type of thinking as well: "The next few days are going to be unbearable," "Boy, am I going to be tired tomorrow," "I just know my meeting is going to be a disaster," "I know my boss and I are going to argue again the next time we meet," "I'm dreading training that new employee." There are endless variations of this stressful tendency. The details are usually different, but the result is the same—stress!

"I used to worry so much about my upcoming annual reviews," said Janet, a comptroller at an auto parts manufacturer. "Finally I decided I had to break my habit. My worry was eating me up and draining my energy. I realized that only once in fifteen years had I been given a negative review—and even then, nothing bad happened. What's the point of worry anyway? What we worry about rarely happens, and even when it does, the worry doesn't help."

Gary, a restaurant manager, described himself as a "world-class worrywart." Every night, he anticipated the worst—hostile or dissatisfied customers, stolen food, contaminated meat, an empty room— "You name it, I worried about it." At the time, he considered himself somewhat wise, as if his anticipatory thinking would head off certain negative events. After many years of anticipating the worst, however, he concluded that, in reality, the opposite was true. He began to see that his worrisome thinking would, in some cases, create problems that weren't really there. To quote Gary, "I would work myself up into a lather and get really upset. Then, because I was anticipating the worst and expecting everyone to make mistakes, I'd be unforgiving of really minor things—a waitress would mix up an order and I'd chew her out. She would become so upset and worried that she'd start making much more serious mistakes. Looking back, most of it was my own fault."

Obviously, some planning, anticipating, and looking forward to future events and accomplishments are an important and necessary part of success. You need to know where you'd like to go in order to get there. However, most of us take this planning far too seriously and engage in futuristic thinking far too often. We sacrifice the actual moments of life in exchange for moments that exist only in our imaginations. An imagined future may or may not ever come true.

Sometimes people ask me, "Isn't it exhausting and unbearable being on a promotional tour—a new city every single day, living out of a suitcase for weeks at a time?" I admit that occasionally I do get really tired, and sometimes I even complain about it, but in reality it's a lot of fun as long as I take it one event at a time. If I spend a great deal of time and energy, however, thinking about how many interviews I have tomorrow, my next ten public appearances, or tonight's long airplane flight, it's predictable that I'll be exhausted and overwhelmed. Whenever we focus too much on all there is to do instead of simply doing what we can in this moment, we will feel the stress associated with such thinking.

The solution for all of us is identical. Whether you're dreading tomorrow's meeting, or next week's deadline, the trick is to observe your own thoughts caught up in the negative expectations and imagined horrors of the future. Once you make the connection between your own thoughts and your stressful feelings, you'll be able to step back and recognize that if you can rein in your thoughts, bringing them back to what you are actually doing—right now—you'll have far more control over your stress level.

45

Admit That It's Your Choice

This can be a difficult strategy to embrace. So many people resist it, yet if you can embrace it, your life can begin to change—immediately. You will begin to feel more empowered, less victimized, and as if you have more control of your life. Not a bad set of rewards for a simple admission of the truth.

The admission I'm referring to is your choice of career and the accompanying hassles. You must admit that, despite the problems, limitations, obstacles, long hours, difficult coworkers, political aspects, sacrifices you make, and all the rest, you are doing what you are doing because you have made the choice to do so.

"Wait a minute," I've been told so many times, "I'm doing what I'm doing, not by choice, but because I have to. I have no choice." I know it can seem that way. Yet if you think through this issue in a reflective way, you'll begin to see that in reality it really is your choice.

When I suggest that you admit that your job or career is your choice, I'm not saying that your problems are necessarily your fault, or that it's realistic that you make other choices. What I am suggesting is that ultimately, all things considered (including necessity, lifestyle choices, income needs, and the possibility of losing your job or even your home), you've made the decision to do what you're doing. You have weighed the options, considered your alternatives, studied the consequences, and, after all is said and done, you've decided that your best alternative is to do exactly what you are doing.

Chris, who works for a large advertising firm, resented this suggestion. In a bitter tone of voice, he told me, "That's absolutely ridiculous. I'm not choosing to work twelve hours a day on these stupid campaigns; I'm forced to. If I didn't work so hard, I'd be blackballed as lazy and go nowhere in this business or in the entire industry."

Can you see what a corner this man had painted himself into? Despite being a bright, up-and-coming advertising account executive, he felt trapped and resentful, a victim of "the way things have to be." He felt absolutely out of the loop when it came to taking any responsibility for his career choices and how hard he was working. The problem is, when you feel trapped and as if you aren't making your own choices, you feel like a victim.

Despite his objections, Chris had decided that it was worth it to work twelve hours a day. His decision was that, all things considered, he'd rather stay in his current position than go through the hassles, risk, and fear of looking for another job, making less money, losing his prestige, missing out on his chance to advance his career, and so forth. I can't tell you if his decision was a good one or not, but isn't it obvious that this was his choice?

Megan, a single mother, had a full-time job as a nurse, but dreamed of becoming a hospital administrator. When I met her at a book signing, she confessed to having spent the previous eight years convincing herself that she was a victim. Frequently, she would tell others, "I'd love to pursue my dream but it's impossible—look at my life."

Despite the very real difficulties she was facing, her greatest obstacle was her unwillingness to admit that her profession was her choice, as was her decision to stay right where she was. She had access to a good school, the grades to be admitted, and some good

friends who would help her out with her daughter. None of that mattered, however, because she was a single mom.

The way she described her transformation, one of her friends had convinced her to stop blaming her circumstances. Somehow, she listened, and had the humility to make the change.

The way she put it, "The moment I admitted that *I* was the choice-maker, everything fell into place. I was able to enroll in the part-time night school program, and I'm already a third of the way through. It's frightening to think about how much I was getting in my own way. I realized that I may be a single mom for the rest of my life."

From time to time, most of us fall into the trap of believing that our circumstances are entirely beyond our control. Taking responsibility for your choices, however, takes you out of any "poor me" thinking and into an empowering, "I'm in charge of my own life" mind-set. I hope you'll reflect on this strategy because I'm confident that if you do, you'll feel less stressed and significantly more successful.

46

Learn to Delegate

For obvious reasons, learning to be a better delegator can make your life easier. When you allow others to help you, when you put your faith in them and trust them, it frees you up to do what you do best.

I've found, however, that many people—even very high-achieving, talented, and successful people—are often very poor delegators. The feeling is, "I might as well do it myself—I can do it better than anyone else." There are several major problems with this attitude. First of all, no one can do all things or be two places at once. Sooner or later, the magnitude of responsibility will catch up with you. Because you're so scattered, you'll be doing a lot of things, but the quality of your work will suffer. Learning to delegate helps to solve this problem by keeping you focused on what you're most qualified to do and that which you enjoy doing. In addition, when you don't delegate properly, you aren't allowing others the privilege of showing you what they can do. So, in a way, it's a little selfish.

Jennifer is a mortgage broker in a busy downtown office. Ironically, one of her biggest problems may have been that she was talented and highly competent at practically everything! She felt so secure about her ability to accomplish tasks, that she had become frightened at delegating almost any authority or responsibility. Whether it was making phone calls, negotiating with lenders, com-

municating with clients, or filling out paperwork, she was involved and on top of it all.

For a while, she managed to juggle things pretty well. As the years went by, however, and her time became more in demand, her unwillingness to delegate responsibility began to catch up with her. She was making more mistakes and becoming increasingly frustrated, forgetful, and stressed out. The people she worked with claimed she had become more short-tempered and arrogant.

At a seminar designed to help her prioritize more effectively, it became obvious to her that her greatest professional weakness was her unwillingness to delegate and share responsibility. She learned the obvious—-that no one can do everything indefinitely, and keep doing it well.

As she began to delegate responsibility—little things as well as those more important—she began to see light at the end of the tunnel. Her mind calmed down, and she began to relax. She could see more clearly where her talent could be used and where her time was best spent. She told me, "I'm back to my old self again."

Often it not only helps you but someone else when you delegate at work. When you ask for help, share responsibility, or delegate authority, you are often giving someone a chance to show you, or someone else, what they can do. In the publishing world, a senior editor might allow an associate editor to do some editing on a particular book, even though it's one of her favorite authors. This not only frees the senior editor's time, it also gives the associate editor a chance to show what she can do—so that she can enhance her career. My friends in the legal and corporate worlds say it works in the same way. Partners in law firms delegate a great deal of work to younger lawyers. Managers of corporations do the same to their less-experienced coworkers. I know that a cynic will say, "The only reason people delegate is to shove off the tough and dirty work on others." And, yes, there are plenty of people who look at it that way—but you don't have to. The point is, there are good reasons—in addition to selfish ones—to practice delegation.

I've seen flight attendants who are masters at delegation. Somehow they are able to get everyone working as a team, so that everyone's job is a bit easier. I've seen others who insist on doing everything themselves. They are the ones who seem the most stressed, and who make the passengers wait the longest. I've seen great chefs delegate certain chores—chopping, for instance—not because they don't like to do it, but because it allows them to focus on other aspects of food preparation that they excel at.

Whether you work in a restaurant, office, airport, retail outlet, or practically anywhere else, learning to delegate can and will make your life a bit easier. Obviously, there are select professions and positions that don't lend themselves well to delegation. For a good number of people, there's no way to say, "Here, you do it." If you fall into this category, perhaps you can practice at home. Can your spouse or roommate help you? Can you delegate certain chores to your kids? Might it be a good idea to hire someone to clean your home, change your oil, or something else that is time-consuming? If you think about your specific circumstances, you'll probably be able to think of at least a few ways to become a better delegator. If you do, you'll free up some time and make your life easier.

47

Take Your Next Vacation at Home

This is a strategy I began using a number of years ago. To be honest, the first few times I gave it a try, I felt sure I was going to be giving up something—fun, relaxation, "my big chance to get away"—and that I would end up disappointed. However, I can honestly say that every time I have stayed home for my vacation, I'm really glad I did. Never once have I regretted my decision.

Vacations are something most people look forward to. They are usually wonderful, well-deserved, and almost always needed. However, a vacation which is ideally designed to be relaxing, rejuvenating, and energizing can at times bring on more stress than it eliminates. Here's a scenario. You finally get a week off. You have a great trip planned, yet you still have to do all that's necessary to leave. You rush to pack and to get all the loose ends and assorted details attended to. You're exhausted. It feels like you haven't had a chance to sit still for weeks. Yet here you are, running to catch another airplane, or rushing out the door to avoid traffic. In a way it seems like you're *speeding up so that you can slow down.* You want to get the most out of your vacation, so you won't be back until late next Sunday night—so you can start work again early the next day. Even before you leave, you know it's going to be tough coming back.

Part of you can't wait to leave because you know you're going to have a great time and get away from your normal routine—but the other part would love the chance to piddle around the house, curl up with a great book, start that yoga or exercise program, or maybe take a couple of simple, but relaxing day trips closer to home. But all that will have to wait because you're going on vacation.

Unfortunately, that other part of you—the part that would love to turn off the phone, play with the kids, clean the closet, avoid crowds, read a book, jog or walk through a local park, plant a garden—rarely, if ever, gets a chance to be nurtured. Your normal life keeps you way too busy, or you're on vacation away from home.

Kris and I had a great home based vacation several years ago. We agreed that work was off limits—even for one minute during the week. No work-related phone calls would be made or returned—just like we were on vacation. As far as we (and everyone else) were concerned, we *were* on vacation. We turned the ringer on the phone to the "off" position.

We hired a baby-sitter (the kids' favorite person, to make it fun for them) to play with the kids every morning for a few hours while we went jogging together, did yoga, or went out to breakfast. We did several little home projects we had wanted to do for years. We worked in the garden. We sat in the sun and read. It was heavenly. In the afternoons, we did something really fun as a family—hiking, swimming, or hide-and-seek. One day, we hired a massage therapist to give us back-to-back massages, and every night we had different take-out for dinner. We had someone come to the house and help us with the cleaning and laundry—just like being at a hotel. We saw several great movies and we slept in every day. It was like having nine Sundays back to back at a great hotel—at a tiny fraction of the cost!

The kids had a blast, and so did we. We felt as if we finally had the chance to really enjoy our home as a family. The kids were able to see their parents not rushed, at home. (What a concept!) I was more relaxed and rested than I ever remember being after going away for a vacation. And it was so much easier, not only to plan, but to get back into the swing of things once I was back—no travel delays, no lost bags, no jet lag, and no exhaustion from traveling with kids. Because we thought of it as a vacation, we lived like royalty that week—massages, restaurants, a house cleaner, take-out—yet we spent a fraction of what we would have spent flying or even driving to some exotic vacation or fancy hotel. But more than all of that, it was truly special. We realized we work so hard to have a home and to care for it—yet it's so rare that we get to enjoy it without being in a hurry.

I'm not advocating replacing all traditional vacations. I love to go away, and I suspect you do too. I can tell you, however, that this is a great way to relax, as well as a chance to do things you almost never get to do at or close to home, while spending very little money. As I look at my calendar, I can see that we have another one of these home vacations coming up soon. I can hardly wait.

48

Put Your Mind in Neutral

One of the first observations I made when I learned to meditate was that my life seemed to calm down. Although I had the same number of things to do, the same responsibilities, and identical problems to deal with, I felt as if I had more time, which made my work life become easier and more enjoyable. I was still surrounded by chaos, but not as adversely affected by it.

While meditation isn't for everyone, there is a reasonable substitute that can be of tremendous help to anyone wishing to become calmer, less reactive, and more peaceful. It involves learning to put your mind in neutral, which you might think of as a form of "active meditation." In other words, unlike some forms of traditional meditation where you sit down, close your eyes, and focus on your breath, active meditation is something you can incorporate into your daily life. The truth is, there are select times you already engage in this process but because it doesn't seem like much, you probably disregard it as insignificant. Therefore, you never learn to use its power.

Essentially, putting your mind in neutral means clearing your mind of focused thinking. Rather than actively thinking, your mind is in a more passive or relaxed state. When your mind is in neutral, your experience of thought is effortless, yet completely responsive to whatever is happening in the moment. Great teachers, for example, or public speakers, will often describe "being on" or "being in the zone" as those times when their thinking is very relaxed, when they aren't forcing the issue.

My best writing is always produced when my mind is in neutral, when I'm not "trying." As I clear my mind, it's almost as though the writing is done for me. Rather than actively pursuing ideas, the thoughts I need and the best ways to express them come to me or "through me." You may notice that when you suddenly remember an important phone number, a person's name, or a forgotten combination, or when you suddenly have an idea that solves a problem, or when you remember where you put your keys, it's your usually relaxed "neutral thinking" that provides the insight or sudden surge of memory. You'll have a "That's it!" moment. At times like these, the harder you try, the less is achieved. It's this effortless quality that is so critical and helpful. Once you start trying or focusing your thinking, you put yourself back into your more normal or analytical thinking.

The reason most people don't consciously use neutral thinking is because they don't recognize its power, or necessarily even consider it to be a form of thinking—but it is. It's taken for granted, seldom used, and almost always overlooked. However, although it's relaxing and de-stressing, it's also very powerful. When your mind is in neutral, thoughts seem to come to you as if out of the blue. New ideas and insights become a way of life because your mind, when it's relaxed, becomes open and receptive to your wisdom and unique greatness.

Obviously, there are times when it's inappropriate or impractical to put your mind in neutral. When your task requires focused concentration, or when you're learning something brand new, it's often in your best interest to think in a more traditional, analytical mode. You'll be amazed, however, at how powerful this process really is—and how much easier your life can become when you learn to incorporate neutral thinking into your daily life. Whenever you feel highly stressed or as though you're expending too much mental energy, it's a good idea to check in with yourself and decide if a little neutral thinking might be just what you need. You can use neutral thinking as a stress-reducing tool, as a way to relax, or as a way to bring forth greater creativity. The applications are virtually unlimited.

To put your mind in neutral is surprisingly simple. You can only be in one mode of thinking or the other—neutral or active. Like a walkie-talkie, you are either on "talk" or "listen," but never both at the same time. So, as you let go or back off of your analytical thinking, your mind automatically shifts into neutral. Once you accept neutral as a viable form of thinking, the rest is easy. I hope you'll experiment with backing off your thinking and quieting your mind. Soon you'll be more relaxed than you could have ever imagined.

49

Remember the Whole Story

I predict that if you experiment with this strategy, you'll begin to realize that in most cases, your life isn't quite as bad as you can sometimes make it out to be. This in turn will heighten your perspective and enjoyment surrounding your work, and help you relax and reduce your stress.

As you probably know, it's extremely seductive, when sharing with others about your workday, to focus primarily on the negative. A fairly typical response to the question, "How was your day?" is, "I had a really tough one." If you elaborate, it's likely that you'll focus on how little time you had, your nightmare commute, the tough issues and conflicts, problems, difficult people, hassles, your sense of hurry and being rushed, negative coworkers, all the things that went wrong, and your demanding boss. And to a certain degree, you're probably right on the mark. For most people, a typical workday is really tough and often downright exhausting. But is this negative assessment the whole story—or is it only part of it? Are you recharacterizing your day the way it actually was—or are you being selective in what you choose to remember and discuss?

I encourage you to be completely honest with yourself as you ponder the following questions about your latest workday: On your way to work, did you stop for a bagel and coffee? Did you take a lunch break? If so, who were you with? Was it enjoyable? How was the food? Did you have any stimulating conversations during the day? Any new insights? Did you have a chance to express your creativity? Did you see any pretty sights or nature—a waterfall in your courtyard, trees and flowers, birds or animals? Did you hear any good jokes today? Did anyone give you a compliment? Did you listen to any good music in the car or perhaps an interesting talk show? Did your in-basket get any smaller? Did you resolve any conflicts? Are you being paid?

I'm not trying to get you to become unrealistically happy. As I mentioned above, I'm well aware that work can be (and often is) difficult. Yet let's not forget that if you answered any of the questions above with a positive response, your day was brighter than a vast majority of the world's population. This doesn't mean you should pretend that you had a wonderful day—yet isn't it easy to take the nice parts of your day completely for granted? We treat them as if they never happened, as if we had no perks, simple pleasures, or conveniences. Indeed, when you examine the above questions, it becomes clear that, for most of us, our day is not entirely negative—or even close to it. If this is the case, why do we describe it as such?

I think there are several reasons. First of all, many of us want to either impress others with our busyness or difficult life, or we are seeking sympathy. Rarely will you hear either spouse say to each other after a long day at work, "I had a terrific day. Lots of things went right." The fear is that to do so (even if it were true) might be seen as a weakness—as if your life were too easy. I know for a fact that some men complain to their wives about how difficult their workday is, in part, because they don't want to be expected to do too much once they get home!

In addition, most of us want to be appreciated and respected for how hard we work. By sharing all that went right during the day, the fear is that we might lose some of that appreciation or respect, and be taken for granted.

But more than all of that, focusing on the negative is just a bad habit—plain and simple. Complaining is contagious, and everyone seems to do it. So, unless you make a conscious effort to do less of it, you're probably going to continue for as long as you are working.

Since I began focusing more on the best parts of my day, my eyes have been opened to a whole new world. I've become increasingly aware that there are all sorts of interesting and enjoyable aspects to my day that were virtually invisible to me prior to this shift in focus. I no longer take for granted those stimulating conversations, interesting challenges, personal contact with friends and others. Perhaps most of all, my appreciation has been heightened. Because of this, I find myself less bothered and annoyed by the hassles and all the "small stuff" that I must deal with on a daily basis. I'm sure the same will be true for you.

50

Don't Live for Retirement

Knowingly or unknowingly, many people practically live for retirement. They think about how wonderful life will be without the burden of daily work outside the home. Some people go so far as to count the years, months, even days before retirement. It's common for people to postpone joy, contentment, and satisfaction until "later." It's almost as though people are "putting in time" as if they were serving a sentence, patiently waiting for their freedom.

Admittedly, most people don't go quite this far. It's usually a bit more subtle than this. However, a staggering percentage of people expect that life down the road is going to be better than it is today. Frequently, daydreams as well as conversations with coworkers and friends make it clear that the expectation is that "someday" will be better than now—when you're retired, have more money, freedom, wisdom, time to travel, or whatever.

I'm passionate about this topic because it's clear to me that thinking in these "someday life will be better" terms is a guaranteed way to set yourself up for a long and tiring career. Rather than enjoying each day, being open to new challenges and opportunities, sharing your gifts with others, and being willing to learn from and become inspired by your work-related experiences, you choose instead to essentially put your life on hold, to go through the motions, get stuck in a rut, and, to one degree or another, feel sorry for yourself.

It's far better, I believe, to wake up each morning and remind yourself of the old adage, "Today is the first day of the rest of my life." Make the decision to honor your gift of life by giving today your best effort, regardless of what you happen to do for a living. See if you can keep perspective when others may not, inspire another person, or make a contribution, however small, to the life of someone else. Remind yourself that all days were created equal, that today is every bit as important as any future day after retirement.

Another important reason to avoid living for retirement is that doing so increases the likelihood that you'll be disappointed when it arrives. A strange thing happens when we postpone happiness until a later date. It's as though, in the meantime, we're rehearsing how to be unhappy. We become experts. When we tell ourselves we'll be happy later, what we're really saying is that our life isn't good enough right now. We have to wait until our circumstances are different. So we wait and wait. Thousands of times, over the course of many years, we remind ourselves, in the privacy of our own minds, that when things are different—someday down the road—we'll feel satisfied and happy. But for now, we'll have to make do.

Finally, the big day arrives—the first day of retirement. Yippee!

But here's the problem. As you probably know, old habits die hard. If you smoke or stutter, it's difficult to quit. If you're highly critical or defensive, it's hard to change. If you have bad eating and exercise habits, it takes enormous discipline to make a permanent shift. In the vast majority of cases, most people simply can't do it. It's too hard to change.

Why in the world do we assume that our thinking habits are any different? They're not. In fact, in some ways, learning to think differently is the most difficult habit of all to change. All of us have been trapped from time to time by our own thinking. We become accustomed to thinking in a certain way—so much so, we can't see it any other way.

If you spend years and years thinking that life isn't good enough right now—that something else is going to be better—it's ludicrous to believe that in a single moment when retirement becomes reality, you're going to somehow begin to think differently; that somehow life as it is is suddenly going to be good enough. No way. It's not going to happen. Instead, it's predictable that the opposite will happen. Your mind will continue to believe that something else will be better. You have a habit of seeing life this way, and it's not going to stop simply because your external life has shifted.

The way around this problem is to commit to being happy now— to make the absolute best of the job or career you have right now, to see it as an adventure, to be creative and insightful. Make this your habitual way of thinking about your job and of being in the world. Practice this type of healthy, optimistic thinking on a day-to-day, moment-to-moment basis. If you do, then when retirement arrives, whether it's a year from now or twenty years from now, you will know the secret of happiness: that there is no way to happiness; happiness *is* the way. It will be second nature to you.

So, go ahead and look forward to a fantastic retirement. Plan ahead and plan well. But do yourself a great big favor. Don't miss a single day along the way. I will conclude by saying that I hope this section has been helpful to you and that I send you my love, respect, and best wishes.

Treasure yourself.

DON'T SWEAT THE SMALL STUFF
WITH YOUR FAMILY

51

Set a Positive Emotional Climate

Just like a garden that flourishes best under certain conditions, your home operates more smoothly when the emotional climate is well thought out. Rather than simply reacting to each crisis and circumstance as it arises, setting an emotional climate gives you a head start in fending off potential sources of stress and conflict. It helps you respond to life rather than react to it.

When trying to determine the ideal emotional environment for yourself and/or your family, there are several important questions to ask yourself: What type of person are you? What type of environment do you enjoy and thrive in? Do you wish your home were more peaceful? These types of questions are critical in order to set the optimal emotional climate.

The creation of an emotional climate has more to do with your inner preferences than your external environment. For example, the placement of your furniture or the colors of your walls or carpet can contribute to the emotional environment but are not the most critical ingredients. Your emotional environment is primarily made up of things like noise levels, the speed of activity (is everyone rushing around like a chicken with its head cut off?), the respect of one another, and the willingness (or lack of willingness) to sit still and listen.

In our home, for example, we have determined that our goal is to create and maintain an environment of relative calm. Although we often fall short of our goal, we do take steps to put the odds in our favor. For example, although we all love spending time together, and we very often do, each of us also enjoys spending time alone in our home. The simple recognition that being alone is thought of as positive, rather than as negative, makes it easier for all of us to be sensitive to the noise, activity, and chaos levels that are occurring at any given moment. We have learned to sense when one of us needs a quieter environment or the space to be alone.

Another thing we try to do is to keep unnecessary rushing around to a minimum. Even though our children are only eight and five years old, we have discussed this issue many times. As a family, we have agreed to work on this tendency as individuals as well as in our interactions together. For example, if I fall into my habit of rushing around, trying to do too many things at once, I've given my children permission to gently remind me to slow down. They know that keeping a sane pace is important to the quality of our life at home and they feel comfortable reminding me when I'm interfering with this goal.

Obviously, the ideal emotional environment is going to be different from home to home. However, I think you'll find that if you spend a little time reflecting on what type of environment you would most prefer, you'll see relatively simple changes that you can begin to implement. Be patient with this one. It may have taken many years to create your current emotional environment, so it may take a little time to create a new one. Over time, I'm fairly certain you'll find this strategy extremely rewarding.

52

Give Yourself an Extra
Ten Minutes

When you ask a typical person or family about what stresses them out the most, it's rare that someone doesn't include the fact that they are almost always running "a few minutes behind." Whether you're off to a soccer match, work, the airport, a neighborhood picnic, a typical day at school, or church, it seems that most of us almost always find a way to wait until the last possible minute to leave, thus running a little late. This tendency creates a great deal of unnecessary stress as we're constantly thinking about who is waiting for us, how far we are behind schedule, and how often this occurs. Invariably, we end up clutching the steering wheel, tightening our neck, and worrying about the consequences of being late. Running late makes us feel stressed out and encourages us to sweat the small stuff!

This ever-so-common problem is easily solved by simply giving yourself an extra ten minutes to get yourself and your family to your appointments. Irrespective of where you're headed, tell yourself that, no matter what, you're going to be ten minutes *early* instead of waiting until the last possible moment to rush out the door.

The key, of course, is to start getting ready a little earlier than usual and to be sure you're all-the-way ready before you start doing something else. I can't tell you how much this simple strategy has helped me in my own life. Rather than constantly scrambling to find my daughters' shoes or my wallet at the last possible moment, I'm now usually ready with plenty of time to spare. Don't kid yourself that these extra ten minutes aren't significant—they are. The extra few minutes before and between activities can be the difference between a stressful day and a joyful day. In addition, you'll discover that when you're not running late you'll be able to enjoy rather than rush through the different things you do each day. Even simple, ordinary events can be great fun when you're not in such a hurry.

When you're done with one activity, leave a little earlier for the next one. When possible, try to schedule your activities, work, play, and everything else a little further apart. Finally, don't overschedule. Allow for some downtime, time where absolutely nothing is scheduled.

If you implement this strategy, you'll be amazed at how much more relaxed your life will seem. The constant sense of pressure, of rushing around, scrambling, will be replaced with a quiet sense of peace.

53

Listen to Her (and Him Too)

If I had to pick a single suggestion that was designed to help virtually all relationship and family problems, it would be to become a better listener. And although a vast majority of us need a great deal of work in this area, I'd have to say that it's us *men* who need it the most!

Of the hundreds of women I've known over my lifetime, and the thousands I've spoken to through my work, a vast majority complain that a spouse, boyfriend, significant other, or father is a poor listener. And most say that the slightest improvement in the quality of listening would be extremely well received and would undoubtedly make the relationship, regardless of the nature of the relationship, even better. Listening is almost like a "magic pill" that is virtually guaranteed to produce results.

It's interesting to speak to couples who claim they have a loving relationship. In most cases, if you ask them the secret of their success, they will point to the other person's ability to listen as one of the most significant factors that contributes to the quality of their relationship. This is also true of positive father/daughter, as well as boyfriend/girlfriend, relationships.

Why, then, if the payback is so powerful and certain, do so few of us become good listeners? There are a few reasons that stick out in my mind. First, as far as men are concerned, many of us feel that listening is a nonproactive solution. In other words, when we're listening instead of jumping in, we don't feel as though we're doing anything. We feel we're being too passive. It's hard for us to accept the fact that the listening itself is the solution.

The way to overcome this particular hurdle is to begin to understand how much being listened to is valued by the people we love. When someone genuinely listens to us, it feels as though we are heard and loved. It nourishes our spirits and makes us feel understood. On the other hand, when we don't feel listened to, our hearts sink. We feel as though something is missing; we feel incomplete and dissatisfied.

The other major reason so few of us become good listeners is that we don't realize how bad we really are! But, other than someone telling us about it or pointing it out to us in some way, how would we know? Our poor listening skills become an invisible habit that we don't even realize we have. And because we have so much company, our listening skills probably seem more than adequate—so we don't give it much thought.

Determining how effective you are as a listener takes a great deal of honesty and humility. You have to be willing to quiet down and listen to yourself as you jump in and interrupt someone. Or you have to be a little more patient and observe yourself as you walk away, or begin thinking of something else, before the person you are speaking to has finished.

This is about as close as you're going to get to a virtually guaranteed result. You may be amazed at how quickly old problems and issues correct themselves and how much closer you will feel to the ones you love if you simply quiet down and become a better listener. Becoming a better listener is an art form, yet it's not at all complicated. Mostly, all it requires is your intention to become a better listener, followed by a little practice. I'm sure your effort will be well worth it!

Don't Answer the Phone

How often have you been completely overwhelmed by all that you're doing at home when, at the worst possible moment, the phone rings? Or, you're trying desperately to get out the door by yourself or with your kids when—*ring, ring ring*—the phone calls out for your attention. Or, on the other end of the spectrum, you're absorbed in a special moment—by yourself or with someone you love—when, again, the phone rings.

The question is, did you answer it? If you're like most people, you probably did. But why? Our response to a ringing phone is one of the few things in life over which we have absolute control and decision-making authority. In this day and age of answering machines and voice mail, it's not as critical to answer the phone as it once was. In most cases, we can simply call someone back at a more convenient time.

In our home, one of the most stressful moments is when the phone rings just as we are going out the door in the morning and one of the kids runs over and answers it! Now, rather than getting in the car, I'm back on the phone addressing someone else's concern. The time and accompanying stress is rarely worth it. I've learned a little secret. I have one of those phones that has a "ringer off" feature. Sometimes, when I remember, I turn the ringer off about thirty minutes before we actually have to leave. This way, the kids won't be tempted to answer the phone.

Many years ago a good friend of mine and I were talking about the issue of answering the phone during a family dinner. We agreed that unless you were expecting a very important call, answering the phone during family time sends a hurtful message to your entire family and is, in fact, disrespectful. The message is: An unknown person is calling and it's more important to me that I answer his or her call than it is to sit with you right now. Pretty scary, isn't it?

Some of my most magical moments with my kids have been when we've been spending time together reading or playing and the phone rings. But rather than interrupting our time together, we look at each other and agree—nothing is more important than our time together right now! This is one of the ways I show my kids how important they are to me. They know I practically live on the phone and my decision to not answer it doesn't come easily.

Obviously there will be many times when you'll want to answer the phone. I urge you, however, to choose carefully. Ask yourself the question "Is answering the phone at this moment going to make my life easier, or is it going to add stress to my day? Simple as it seems, choosing *not* to answer the phone, on selected occasions, can be a very empowering decision and can greatly reduce the stress in your home life.

Encourage Boredom
in Your Children

To the typical parent, little is more aggravating than hearing these words from their children: "I'm bored" or "There's nothing to do." This is especially true for parents who try really hard to provide their children with a variety of experiences and activities to choose from. Yet, ironically, it's the parents who try the hardest who usually suffer the most from these words.

Children who have too many opportunities, choices, scheduled activities, and things to do are often the ones who are the most susceptible to boredom. The reason is that these children are used to being entertained and stimulated virtually every moment of every day. They often rush from activity to activity with little time in between and have schedules that look almost as full as those of their parents! Very simply, if something isn't going on, they feel bored and restless, almost desperate to find something to do. Many kids feel they can't live without a telephone in their hand, a television set or radio playing at virtually every moment, or a computer or video game to entertain them.

The solution *isn't* to feed them ideas of things that they can do to alleviate their boredom. As you know, they will usually reject your ideas anyway. A bigger issue, however, is that in the long run you're doing a disservice to your kids. By offering too many suggestions about ways to keep busy, you are actually feeding the problem by suggesting that the kids really *do* need something to do every minute of every day.

A great solution (and one that will shock your bored kids) is to respond to the "I'm bored" line with a confident "Great, be bored." You can even go on and say "It's good for you to be bored once in a while." I can almost guarantee you that, once you try this a few times and really mean it, your kids will give up on the idea that it's *your* responsibility to entertain them on an ongoing basis. A hidden benefit to this strategy is that it will encourage greater creativity in your kids by forcing them to discover things to do on their own.

I'm not suggesting you do this all the time or that you don't take a loving, active role in the activities that your kids participate in. What I'm referring to here is a response to overstimulation—when you know in your heart that your kids have plenty of things to do and that their boredom is coming from them, not from a lack of possibilities. I think you'll love the sense of authority you'll feel by putting the problem of boredom back where it belongs—with your kids. And, as important, you'll be doing your kids a tremendous favor by teaching them that there's nothing wrong with not having something to do every minute of every day. It's okay to be bored once in a while.

Expect It to Spill

I learned this trick more than twenty years ago. It has proven day after day, year after year, to be extremely effective in my goal of creating a more peaceful home environment for myself and for others.

The basis for this strategy stems from the understanding that when we expect something to occur, we are less surprised and therefore less reactive to it. In addition, when we expect something to happen—that is, when we expect something to spill—and it doesn't, we feel grateful. In other words, we begin to appreciate the fact that, a vast majority of the time, the things we are eating and drinking don't get all over the floor and, most of the time, life does go smoothly. The problem is, we tend to focus on the annoying exceptions.

Think back to the last time you or someone in your family spilled a glass of milk or a cup of coffee on the carpet. What was your reaction? In all probability, it involved panic, disappointment, and a great deal of stress. What do you suppose would happen if, instead of assuming that nothing should or will ever spill, you instead expected the beverage to spill—you accept it as inevitable? It puts an entirely different slant on the same set of facts. This doesn't mean you like it when the spill occurs, only that it's okay when it does—you accept it. Obviously, you have no idea when the spill is going to occur, only that, in all likelihood, it will at some point. It might be later today, next week, or three years from now, but unless you are a rare exception, you will have spilled milk in your home at some point in the future. This strategy prepares you for this inevitable moment.

The same metaphor can easily be extended to virtually any other likely daily annoyance at home—something doesn't work right, something breaks down, some big mess occurs, someone doesn't do his or her part, whatever! The point is, when you expect something to happen, it won't come as such a surprise when it does. Don't worry that by expecting something to happen you're going to encourage it to take place. You're not. We're not talking about "visualizing" something to happen or encouraging it in any way. We're referring here to the gift of acceptance, learning to accept things as they are instead of pinning our happiness on the way we demand things to be. Watch what happens when you expect something to spill. I'll bet you'll find yourself far more relaxed the next time it occurs.

Allow "White Space" in Your Calendar

Too much of anything, even good things, is just that—too much! Regardless of how social you are—or how much you love spending time with others—there is something magical and peaceful about looking at your calendar and seeing white space, *un*-planned-for time. "White space" is time for you to catch up, or to do nothing at all. Creating blocks of time in your calendar where absolutely nothing is planned contributes to a feeling of peace, the feeling that you have enough time.

If you wait for everything to get done before you allow time for yourself, you'll rarely, if ever, find it. Instead, your calendar and schedule will miraculously fill up with your own commitments, as well as with the needs and requests of others. Your spouse or partner will have things for you to do, your kids (if you have them) will have no trouble firing requests at you, as will the neighbors, your friends, and family. Then there are the social commitments—some you love, others agreed to out of obligation. Many other requests, of course, come at you from work as well as from strangers such as telephone solicitors and salespeople. It seems that everyone wants and gets a piece of your time. Everyone, that is, except you.

The *only* solution seems to be to schedule time for yourself with the same degree of respect and commitment that you would schedule an appointment with your doctor or best friend. You make an appointment and, short of an emergency, you keep it! The procedure itself is very simple. You look at your calendar and schedule (in pen) time for yourself. You need to cross out blocks of time where you don't allow anything to be formally scheduled.

As I look at my own calendar, I'm noticing that I have time for myself scheduled this Friday between 1:30 and 4:30 P.M. There is *nothing* scheduled during that time and, short of an emergency, nothing will be. This means that when someone asks me to do something during that time block—a radio show wants an interview, someone wants me to call, a client needs my help, whatever—I can't do it. I've already got plans! And those plans are with myself. Later this month, I have an entire day blocked out. This, too, is sacred time, and I can almost guarantee that it won't be filled up.

As you can imagine, this takes some getting used to. When I first started scheduling time for myself a few years back, I used to have the fear that, as I was taking time for myself, I was missing out on other opportunities or that I would be perceived as selfish. It was very difficult for me to learn to say that I didn't have time when there was that opening in my calendar! What I realized, however, was that I was worth it—and so are you.

This white space time has become one of the most important scheduled activities on my calendar and is something I have learned to protect and value. This doesn't mean my work is any less important to me, or that my time with my family isn't still the most important activity of all. Instead, it simply suggests that my white space time creates a needed degree of balance that nurtures my soul. Without it, life seems too hectic and overwhelming.

I encourage you to start today. Take a look at your calendar and pick a regular time—once a week, even once a month to begin with—even if it's just a few hours, but reserve some time for yourself. Then, as requests come your way, don't even think about putting them in this sacred time slot. Begin to value your time as much as, or more than, anything else. Don't worry. You won't be turning yourself into a selfish person. In fact, just the opposite is likely to occur. As you begin to feel as though your life is your own again, you'll find that you're far more available to the needs of others. When you finally have what *you* need, you'll discover it's easier to give back to others.

Stop Exchanging Horror Stories

This strategy is particularly suited for people who live together. It's a common phenomenon for two people, whether they work away from the home or stay at home during the day, to come together in the evening and spend a great deal of time and energy exchanging "horror stories." More specifically, what I mean is that the bulk of the conversation is geared toward all the rotten and horrible things that went on during the day. Discussions include how difficult and tiring the day was, how many demands were placed on you, the irritations you had to face, the inconveniences, the bad experiences, the difficult moments, the demanding children, the insensitive bosses, and so forth. It seems many of us want to be sure that our spouses or living partners understand how difficult our lives really are.

There are several reasons why I believe this habit is a big mistake. First off, most of us have precious little time to spend each day with our loved ones. It seems to me that, if we have a difficult day, it doesn't make any sense to re-create it in the evening. The act of thinking about and discussing the negative events of the day is tantamount to re-experiencing them. This creates an enormous amount of stress and is emotionally draining.

Second, focusing too much on the negative parts of your day is self-validating. In other words, it serves to remind you of the pressures and difficulties of daily living, thereby convincing you that it's appropriate to be serious, heavyhearted, and uptight.

The simple act of eliminating, or at least reducing, the amount of energy you spend telling your horror stories has an almost instant and in some ways magical quality of making you feel better about your life. It's not that you don't have extremely difficult and serious things to deal with—we all do—it's just that commiserating with others about these difficult parts of life costs far more than it is worth. As you let go of this tendency, you'll be reminded of the better parts of life. It will be easier to remember and think about the loving and kind aspects of life, those things that went right and went well, the parts of your life that you are proud of and that nourish you. You'll also notice that when more of your attention is on the positive aspects of your day, your spouse or living partner will quickly follow suit. Most people, when they break this all-too-common habit, find that focusing on the positive is far more interesting and a great deal more fun. New doors will open in your relationship, and new interests will develop.

Please understand that I'm not suggesting that it's never appropriate or useful to share what's going on—including the worst things—with your loved ones. At times, you may want to, or even need to. There are many exceptions to this strategy. What I'm suggesting you get away from is the abuse of this tendency. Rather than making it a regular part of your evening, something you do without question on a regular basis, see if you can reduce it to an occasional thing that you discuss. Obviously, you want to be honest about your true feelings, but I've found that it can be richly rewarding to leave some of the negative behind. Before jumping in, you might ask yourself, "What is this going to accomplish?" Or you might ask, "Is sharing this information going to brighten either of our days, or is it going to bring us down? Is it going to bring us closer, make us more intimate, or is it going to be one more reminder of how difficult life can be?"

I think we all know that life can be extremely difficult and tiring. I also believe that most of us take it as a given that we must deal with hassles each and every day. The questions are, Does sharing all the gloomy details do any good? Does it have true value? And despite the fact that I'm as guilty as anyone else of abusing this tendency at times, I've found that, a vast majority of the time, sharing negativity is counterproductive at best and an interference to a quality, relaxing evening.

I encourage you to give this suggestion a try. The next time you feel like sharing information on how horrible or testing your day has been, see if you can keep it to yourself instead. My guess is that you'll discover it to be a truly healing thing to do.

59

Never, Ever, Take Your Spouse (or Significant Other) for Granted

I could write an entire book on this subject. But, since I have only a few paragraphs to explain, I'll get right to the heart of the matter.

If you take your spouse for granted, it is absolutely 100 percent guaranteed to adversely affect your relationship. I've never, ever, met a single person who likes to be taken for granted—and very few who will put up with it, over the long run.

Clearly, one of the most disrespectful and destructive things we can possibly do to our spouses (or anyone) is to take them for granted. To do so is sort of like saying, "It's your job to make my life easier and my job to expect it." Ouch!

There are so many ways we take our partners for granted. Here are just a few: We take *our* roles more seriously than theirs. We think our contributions are significant and that our partners are "the lucky ones." Many of us forget to say please and thank-you—some of us never do. We fail to reflect on how lucky we are or how sad and difficult it would be to live without our spouses. Sometimes we get very demanding of our spouses or treat them much differently than we would a friend. Other times, we speak "for them" or disrespectfully about them in front of others. Some of us think we know what our spouses are thinking, so we make decisions for them. Then there is the common mistake of coming to expect certain things—a clean home or a hot meal. Or money to pay the bills, or a nice clean-cut lawn. They are, after all, our spouses. They should do these things. Finally, very few of us really listen to our spouses or share in their excitement—unless, of course, it matches something *we* are interested in. I could go on and on, but you get the point.

Is it any wonder that close to 50 percent of marriages end in divorce and that many of the rest are painful, boring, and/or less than satisfying? Hardly! It's so obvious, but for some reason we keep making the same mistake—we take our partners for granted.

The reverse is also true—almost nothing makes people feel better than feeling as though they are appreciated and valued. Think about how wonderful it felt when you first met your spouse or significant other. It was absolutely wonderful. And a major contributing factor to this feeling of love you shared was that you truly appreciated each other. You said things like "It's so nice to hear from you" and "Thank you for calling." You expressed your appreciation for everything from a simple compliment to the tiniest gift, card, or gesture of kindness. Each chance you had, you expressed your gratitude, and you never took your new love for granted.

Many people believe that it's inevitable that couples will lose their sense of appreciation for one another. Not so! Appreciation is something you have 100 percent control over. If you choose to be grateful and to express your appreciation, you will do so. And the more you do so, the more you'll be in the healthy habit of noticing things to be grateful for—it's a self-fulfilling prophecy.

My wife, Kris, is one of the most appreciative people I've ever known. She's constantly telling me how much she loves me or how lucky she is to be married to me. I try to remember to do the same because that's exactly how I feel. And you know what? Every time she expresses her appreciation toward me, I feel that much more love for her. And she assures me the same is true for her. But we don't do this as a way of getting love, but simply because we both tend to focus on how lucky we are to have one another as a friend and partner.

For example, I'll be away at a speaking engagement and Kris will leave me a sweet message telling me how grateful she is that I'm willing to work so hard for our family. About the same time, I'll leave a message with her, letting her know how grateful I am that she's willing and able to be home with our children, giving them the love they need and deserve, while I'm away. We both honestly feel that the other is making at least an equal sacrifice and that, regardless, we're on the same team. Then, when she's away and I'm home, it seems that we reverse compliments. She's grateful that I'm willing and able to be at home and I'm equally grateful that she's away making yet another contribution to our family.

Kris and I have been together for more than fifteen years, and we love each other more today than we did all those years ago. I'm absolutely certain that our decision to *not* take each other for granted is one of the major reasons why this is true. I'll bet you'll be shocked at how powerful this strategy can be if you give it a try. For the time being, forget what you are getting back and focus only on what you are giving. I believe that if you make the decision to stop taking your partner for granted, in time your spouse will begin to do the same thing. It feels good to be grateful. Try it, you'll love it!

60

Don't Be a Martyr

Needless to say, we all make many sacrifices and trade-offs in our relationships and family lives. Most of these sacrifices are well worth it. But, as with most things (including good things), too much is still too much.

Obviously, the tolerance levels to stress, responsibility, lack of sleep, sacrifice, hardship, and everything else are going to vary from person to person. In other words, something that's supereasy for you might be quite difficult for me—and vice versa. However, if we can pay attention to, and be honest about, our feelings, each of us knows when the level of stress has risen too high. When it does, we usually feel incredibly frustrated, agitated, and perhaps most of all, resentful. We may feel a little self-righteous and convince ourselves that we're working harder than other people and that we have it tougher than everyone else.

Many of us (myself included) have fallen prey to the seduction of becoming a martyr. It's easy to have this happen because there is often a fine line between working hard out of actual necessity and overdoing it out of perceived necessity.

The sad truth is, however, that no one actually benefits from or appreciates a martyr. To himself, a martyr is his own worst enemy—constantly filling his head with lists of things to do and always reminding himself how difficult his life is. This mental ambush saps the joy from his life. And to the people around him, a martyr is an overly serious complainer who is too self-absorbed to see the beauty of life. Rather than feeling sorry for him, or seeing him as a victim, as the martyr would love to see happen, outsiders usually see a martyr's problems as being completely self-created.

If you think you may have martyr tendencies, I urge you to give them up! Rather than spending 100 percent of your energy doing things for other people, leave something for someone else to do. Take up a hobby. Spend a few minutes a day doing something just for you—something you really enjoy. You'll be amazed by two things. First, you'll actually start to enjoy your life and experience more energy as you feel less stressed. Nothing takes more energy than feeling resentful and victimized. Second, as you let go of resentment and the feeling that everything you do you do out of obligation, the others around you will begin to appreciate you more than before. Rather than feeling as if you resent them, they will feel as if you enjoy and appreciate them instead—which you will. In short, everyone wins and benefits when you give up your victim attitude and your tendency to be a martyr.

61

When Someone Asks You How You Are, Don't Emphasize How Busy You Are

Putting too much emphasis on our busyness has become a way of life, almost a knee-jerk reaction. In fact, I'd guess that one of the most common responses to the greeting "How are you doing?" has become "I'm so busy." As I write about this strategy, I have to admit that, at times, I'm as guilty of this tendency as anyone else. However, I've noticed that as I've become more conscious of it, I'm putting less and less emphasis on my own busyness—and I'm feeling a whole lot better as a result.

It's almost as though we become more comfortable after confirming to others that, we too, are very busy. I was in the grocery story last night on my way home from work when I witnessed two sets of friends greeting one another. The first person said, "Hi, Chuck. How's it going?" Chuck sighed loudly and said, "Really busy, how about you?" His friend responded, "Yeah, me too. I've been working really hard."

Then, almost as if the customers in the store knew I was writing a book, two women added to my material! Not more than a few seconds later, out of the corner of my eye, I heard one woman say to the other, "Grace, nice to see you. How's everything?" Grace's response was to noticeably shrug her shoulders and say, "Pretty good, but really busy," followed by a polite and seemingly sincere "How about you?" The answer: "You know, busy as ever."

It's very tempting to enter into a conversation with these words because the truth is that most of us *are* really busy. Also, many people feel they have to be busy or they have no value in our society. Some people are even competitive about how busy they are. The problem, however, is that this response and overemphasis on how busy we are sets the tone for the rest of the conversation. It puts the emphasis on busyness by reminding both parties how stressful and complicated life has become. So, despite the fact that you have a moment to escape your stressful existence by saying hello to a friend or acquaintance, you are choosing to spend even your spare moments emphasizing and reminding yourself how busy you are.

Despite the fact that this response may have elements of honesty, it works against you—and your friend—by reinforcing your feelings of busyness. True, you're busy, but that's not all you are! You're also an interesting person with many other qualities besides busyness. The fact that most of us emphasize how busy we are to others isn't entirely necessary but is simply a habit many of us have fallen into. We can change this habit by simply recognizing that it exists— and exploring other options.

I think you'll be amazed at how much more relaxed you'll become if you do nothing more than change your initial comments to people you see or talk to on the phone. As an experiment, try to eliminate any discussion about how busy you are for an entire week! It may be difficult, but it will be worth it. You'll notice that, despite being as busy as ever, you'll begin to *feel* slightly less busy. You'll also notice that, as you deemphasize how busy you are, the people you speak to will sense permission from you to place a little less emphasis on their own busyness, helping them to feel a little less stressed and perhaps encouraging your entire conversation to be more nourishing and jointly relaxing. So, the next time someone asks you how you are doing, say anything *except* "I'm really busy." You'll be glad you did.

62

Don't Go to Bed Mad

I learned this bit of wisdom from my parents, and I've appreciated it my entire life. While I was growing up, this family philosophy cut short, or nipped in the bud, many arguments, angry evenings, and negative feelings that would have undoubtedly carried forward to the next day, or perhaps even longer. The idea is that, despite the fact that all families have their share of problems and issues to contend with, nothing is so bad that it's worth going to bed mad over. What this strategy ensures is that, regardless of what's happening, who's to blame, or how mad you or someone else in your family happens to be, there is a set cap or limit to your anger, at which time everyone in the family agrees it's time to let go, forgive, apologize, and start over. No exceptions. This limit is bedtime.

When you have an absolute policy that no one goes to bed mad, it helps you remember that love and forgiveness are never far away. It encourages you to bend a little, to be the first to reach out and open the dialogue, offer a genuine hug, and keep your heart open. When you make the decision to never go to bed mad, it helps you see the innocence in your own behavior and in that of your family members. It keeps the channels of communication open. It reminds you that you are a family and that, despite your problems and disagreements, you love, need, and treasure each other. The decision that it's never a good idea to go to bed mad is a built-in reset button that protects your family from stress, hostility, and resentment.

Perhaps it's easier to see the importance of such a policy in its absence. Without a family policy such as this, arguments and anger are open-ended. No one will have created a boundary, a set of rules that protect your family from extended and unnecessary anger. Without a rule to suggest otherwise, family members can hold on to their anger and justify doing so.

Kris and I have tried very hard to implement this strategy in our family. While it's not perfect, and while occasionally one or more of us seems a little frustrated at bedtime, on balance it's been enormously helpful. It ensures that ninety-nine times out of one hundred, we'll wake up the next morning with love in our hearts and with an attitude of "This is a new day." I hope that you'll give this strategy a fair try. It's certainly not always easy, and you probably won't bat 100 percent, but it's well worth the effort. Remember, life is short. Nothing is so important that it's worth ruining your day, nor is anything so significant that it's worth going to bed mad. Have a nice sleep.

63

Have Family Meetings

The purpose of family meetings is to set up a nondefensive environment in which two or more people who love each other can share freely and communicate from the heart. The idea is to create a "safe place" where everyone present is able to speak and be heard. Everyone agrees, up front, to listen very carefully to everything that is being said. No one is allowed to interrupt, attack, cut someone off, criticize, or butt in before it's his or her turn. No one is better or more important than anyone else. Everyone is treated with respect.

During a family meeting, you are allowed to share what's working for you—and what's not working. You are given permission to share honestly, without being attacked. You can tell the others about things that are bothering you and you can offer potential solutions. You can also share the parts of family life that you love the most and what would make your family even better.

Family meetings are potentially very healing. In our frenzied world, it's often difficult to find the time to sit together as a family to share and listen. Yet, this is a critical component of a loving, functional family. This is an ideal time to be together, to find out what's going on with one another, to stay acquainted, or in some cases, to get acquainted. It's a chance to learn about the other members of your family, to discover what makes them tick and what makes them happy and sad. It's often the case that people discover things about their parents, children, spouses, and siblings that they didn't know. My youngest daughter once told me during a family meeting that when I gave her a certain "look" it made her nervous. Because the purpose of our meeting was to learn from one another in a nondefensive environment, I was able to see exactly what she meant. The "look" she was referring to was one of disapproval. I had no idea I was doing it. If she had brought this up in the midst of a busy day, it's doubtful if I would have been as receptive to her words. But because the whole point of our being together was to improve our family life, I was open and receptive—and able to learn. Since that time, I've been very careful to be aware of my "looks." During our next meeting, I asked her how I was doing, and she said, "Much better." She felt listened to and respected.

I remember a few of the family meetings we had when I was a child. I remember learning of some of the frustrations of my parents. This helped me to see them as people—not just my parents. It helped develop my compassion and perspective.

Family meetings are extremely helpful in venting your frustration as well as reminding you of your shared love for one another. This, in turn, keeps you from "sweating the small stuff" because you won't allow small stuff to build up into big frustrations. Instead, you'll deal with things as they come up. You'll discover solutions that work for the entire family.

Family meetings won't make your life (or your family) perfect. They will, however, keep you much closer as a family. Whether you have two people in your family or ten, I encourage you to give family meetings a try. Your rewards will be significant.

64

Keep Your "Thought Attacks" in Check

In every book I write, and every lecture I give, I try to include a little something on the subject of "thought attacks." Since home is such a potential source of stress for most people, this book will not be an exception.

We are thinking creatures. And because we're constantly thinking, it's easy to forget or at least lose sight of the fact that we are doing so. Instead, when we become lost in thought, our thinking is automatic. In other words, we are thinking about things—how much we have to do, how stressful our lives have become, how often we get stuck with the lion's share of the work, and so on—without conscious awareness that we are actively thinking.

The problem is, our thinking comes back to us in the form of feelings. What I mean by this is that if we're having angry thoughts, we feel angry. If we're having resentful thoughts, we feel resentful. If we're having hurried thoughts, we feel as though we don't have enough time. And if we're having stressful thoughts, we will feel stressed. Don't believe me? Just try to get angry right now without thinking about something that makes you angry! You can't do it. In fact, your feelings follow your thoughts just as surely as a lamb follows its mother.

Typically, a thought attack plays itself out something like this: You have a thought such as "This darn place is never cleaned up." In and of itself, this wouldn't be so harmful. However, we rarely have the wisdom to nip this thought in the bud. Instead, this single thought usually leads to other thoughts like "I'm the only one around here who does anything" and perhaps "I hate this place." Pretty soon, we're bothered and annoyed but don't realize the extent to which our own thinking has contributed to our mental anguish.

When this type of mental conversation takes place, only two things can happen. More often than not, the thinker (you) will continue to think this way until you begin to experience the stressful effects of those thoughts. Your train of thought may continue until you are distracted by a doorbell or a ringing phone.

Another option, however, is to catch yourself in the act of your thought attack—notice what's happening within your own thinking. Say to yourself, "Whoops, there I go again," or something else that reminds you that your thinking is about to drive you crazy and exacerbate any stress you are already feeling. When you become an observer of your own thinking in this manner, it allows you to nip your stress and frustration in the bud by getting you out of your head and back into the present moment. It helps you regain your perspective by not allowing your thoughts to make your life seem even more difficult than it really is. Obviously, the earlier you stop your thought attack, the easier it is to regroup and get back on track.

I can't tell you how useful this simple little technique has been in my own life and in the lives of thousands of others who have given it a try. You'll have fun with this one—but I must warn you. While the concept is simple, it's not always easy to implement. Once you start paying attention, you'll probably discover that you have a lot more thought attacks than you can possibly imagine. But the payoff is worth it. With a little practice, you'll be far more easygoing around the home.

65

Stop Repeating
the Same Mistakes

Many years ago, Australian tennis star Ken Rosewall was asked his secret to success. In this particular interview he responded by saying, "I make a lot of mistakes, but I usually don't repeat them." The confidence he expressed in this answer has always stuck with me. I have found his message to be enormously helpful in my desire to reduce the stress I feel at home.

If you think about it, mistakes are really not that big of a deal. In fact, as most of us acknowledge, we need to make mistakes in order to learn and to grow. The problem, I believe, comes when we are unwilling to either acknowledge or examine the mistakes we make, thus leading to the tendency to repeat them—sometimes over and over.

One of my own ongoing mistakes was my insistence on answering the phone at home regardless of how busy I was. Sometimes I was doing two or three things at once, while already late to take one of the kids to school. Then the phone would ring. Rather than let the answering machine pick it up, I would compound my problem by answering it myself. Now there was someone on the line requiring my attention while everything else was still to be done. The person on the other end of the line would almost always sense my hurry, and would sometimes even ask, "Why did you even bother to pick up the phone?" I must have repeated this mistake hundreds of times before

I finally got it. I have since stopped—and what a tremendous relief it has been! Because I was able to acknowledge the mistake I was making, I was able to make a simple adjustment in my habitual actions. Now, if I'm busy and the phone rings—it simply means the phone is ringing. I won't even consider answering it. This simple change has brought a great deal of peace to what used to be the craziest time of the day.

I've overcome many other repeated mistakes, such as getting too involved in my kids' arguments, trying to fit too many activities into a single day, waiting too long to clean my home office desk, and on and on.

Take a look at your own mistakes. The fact that you make them is no big deal! The more important question is, Are you engaged in *repeated* behavior and mistakes that you might be able to change? In most cases, the answer is yes. I can assure you that it's a very freeing feeling to admit to your mistakes and decide to make a change. That way, you won't be destined to repeat them.

66

Recognize When Someone Doesn't Have an Eye for Something

You may have heard the expression "He doesn't have the eye for it." In case you haven't, it means that the person you are referring to literally can't see what you are talking about; he or she can't understand or internalize it. For example, I remember trying to teach my oldest daughter to add two numbers together. Like the rest of us, before she saw how the principle of addition works in real life, she was stuck using her fingers and anything else necessary to add the numbers together. But, like magic, the moment it clicked, the instant she developed the eye for it, she was on her way.

Needless to say, it would have been foolish (and cruel) to get angry at her for not having the eye for math before she was developmentally ready. Instead, like most caring parents, my wife and I tried to be patient and allow her the necessary time to digest and understand the material.

It's easy to see how relevant having the eye for something is when we're talking about a five- or six-year-old's learning to add. It's something else entirely when we assume that someone should know something, yet it's every bit as important. For example, if you have a sloppy spouse, you probably assume (perhaps incorrectly) that he (or she) truly understands what it means to clean something up—or to live within a budget. You might make similar categorical assumptions about your children over such things as the meaning of quiet, patience, being nice, and other things you and I take for granted. The truth is, however, that many of the things we assume are general knowledge are nothing of the sort. In many instances, the problem *isn't* that a person doesn't want to, or is unwilling to, help but simply that he or she doesn't have the eye for what you are asking him or her to do. It's like you're speaking different languages.

When you take this possibility into consideration, your level of frustration will drop dramatically. Perspective and compassion will replace your demands and judgments. Rather than acting out from a place of stress, you'll be more likely to become a patient teacher, a participant in the process of helping another person develop the eye for something. The person you are dealing with will become much easier to work with. You'll be bringing out the best in him or her, rather than the worst.

My wife had an interesting realization about one of our favorite baby-sitters. Although she was an excellent sitter with the kids, we would come home from a night out and the kitchen would look like a bomb had just struck! We were constantly reminding her to clean up any messes she made, to which she would respond, "No problem." Yet, we'd come home to the same giant mess each and every time. We were getting very frustrated and were considering not using her again when Kris had the insight that the sitter might honestly *not know* what we mean by "clean it all up." To our great surprise, Kris was right. To our baby-sitter, the kitchen was as clean as it needed to be. Apparently, her own kitchen frequently looked messy. It wasn't treated as a big deal in her home. But to us, it was a big deal.

This story has a happy ending. Kris and I spent about thirty minutes showing her exactly what we expected and how to go about it.

To this day, the kitchen has been spotless every time we've come home from a date. The secret wasn't to yell and scream or to get frustrated and fire her—it was to help her develop the eye for a clean kitchen. Experiment with this one and you'll solve many of your day-to-day issues, quickly and easily.

67

Have a Favorite Family Charity

Very few activities can bring a family closer together than the act of giving. We have found that having a favorite family charity is a fun way to do just this. Whether there are just two of you or ten, the idea is to get everyone in your family involved in the selection and ongoing giving process. (Obviously, if you live alone, you can do the same thing by yourself or with a friend.)

Our favorite family charity is Children, Inc., out of Richmond, Virginia; (800) 538-5381. It's an organization ideally suited for this purpose because it's easy to get everyone involved. Your family gets to meet, through the mail, a special child whom you all get to help and, and this is important, get to know. Both you and your kids can send letters, photos, and pictures back and forth to the child you are helping and meet a new friend in the process.

Almost any charity can be an ideal opportunity to bring a family closer together. Rather than simply writing a check and putting it in the mail, bring your family into the process. Get a corporate brochure and show your children who it is you're trying to help and why. Discuss the work that the organization is doing and applaud it together. If you are sending money, let the kids see you write the check. Maybe they can put the check in the envelope, or the envelope in the mailbox. Share with them where the money is going and what it is going to do. Ask your children who they would most like to help and why. Is it children, the elderly, the homeless, or the hungry? Or would they like to make a contribution to the search for the cure for cancer or blindness? Would they like to help stray animals or community development? This strategy gives your family the opportunity to discuss the needs in your community and in our world. It's a demonstration of your love. It's fun and rewarding, as well as helpful.

If you can't afford to give money, your family can still come together around giving. Perhaps your church or local shelter needs some help. A church in our neighborhood makes bag lunches for homeless people every Saturday. What a great way to spend a morning with your family.

What you do isn't as important as doing something. Giving of any kind feels good and brings people together, especially families. I hope you'll give this strategy a try. It will bring your family closer together and reinforce your most important values, and if each family does its own little part, we can make the world a better place.

68

Remind Yourself Frequently What Your Children Really Want

Let's face it. Your kids don't really care if you're a flight attendant, a salesperson, a waitress, a computer expert, or a chef. I can tell you from firsthand experience that they are not impressed if you are an author or a busy professional. My guess is that my kids would be equally *un*-impressed with me if I were a doctor, lawyer, or even a movie star. The fact that you work hard and sacrifice in their behalf may be appreciated, but not nearly to the extent that any of us feel is appropriate and deserved. No, what really matters to kids is your time—and your willingness to listen and love unconditionally. Period!

It's one thing to say "My kids are the most important part of my life," and it's something else altogether to back that statement up with actions. I know this isn't easy, and I also know that there are many great and often legitimate excuses why we can't make our kids our top priority, but the fact remains: Our kids don't want our external successes, they want and need our love.

This is not a strategy designed to make you feel guilty about how little time you have for your kids. Believe me, I often feel guilty myself when I have to leave for the airport before my own children have even gotten out of bed, or when I have to take an important phone call at dinnertime or miss a school play due to other plans. The goal of this strategy is not about guilt, it's about love. It's a friendly reminder that, although parenting can seem overwhelming at times and you might think it will last forever—it won't. Instead, you have a short window of opportunity in which to spend time together and develop a mutually loving and respectful relationship before your children are grown up and out on their own.

At times it's been helpful to me, and I believe it might be helpful to you, to be reminded that what our kids *really* want isn't our money or our success—or our constant reminders of how hard we work. What they really want is us. Obviously, this doesn't mean you don't need to earn a living or that success isn't (or shouldn't be) important, only that, to our kids, these things are secondary. I doubt very much that any of us, on our deathbeds, will wish we had spent even more time at the office or in pursuit of our dreams, but I suspect that many of us will regret not spending more quality time with our children. Knowing this is the case, why not make a change, however slight, in our priorities?

What our children really want (and need) is our love. They want us to listen to their stories without something else on our minds and without rushing to be somewhere else, to watch their soccer games not because we feel obligated to do so but because there is genuinely no place we'd rather be. They want us to hold them, read to them, be with them. They want to be the center of our universe.

Just this morning, I was with a good friend of mine discussing how quickly our children are growing up. It reminded me of how precious my own children, and all children, are. In that moment, I made a commitment to myself to keep my priorities straight, however inconvenient it may be. I hope you'll make a similar commitment.

69

Remember, It's the Little Things That Will Be Remembered Most

Recently, I was in the midst of an extended promotional book tour and had been on some very exciting national television and radio shows. I had been speaking to huge, enthusiastic audiences and was being treated extremely well by my publisher, the public, and everyone else. At the time, I had the #1 best-selling book in America, *Don't Sweat the Small Stuff*, and had been sincerely honored by the reception of my work. Everything was wonderful except one thing—I deeply missed my daily routine of spending time with my family.

One night I called home and my two girls sang to me over the phone, simultaneously telling me how much they loved me and couldn't wait until I got home. They were carving pumpkins for Halloween and promised to save the biggest one for me. As I hung up the phone in the Chicago airport, I began to cry. My tears were a mixture of joy and sadness, of being so deeply touched in the heart that I couldn't contain my emotions. I realized that no matter how wonderful your life is, what your hopes and dreams might be, or what's happening in your career and other aspects of your life, it's the little things that matter most.

That night, as I flew to Hartford, Connecticut, for another show,

I reflected on my fondest memories. And guess what? They weren't our most exciting vacations or my greatest achievements. Although these external things are important to me, the memories that really stand out are those that touched my heart—like the time I was really upset about something and my youngest daughter, Kenna, sensed my emotion and gave me a big bear hug and told me, "Daddy, everything is going to be all right." She was four years old. Nearly two years later, it's as if I can still feel that hug and hear her words of encouragement. Then there was the time my daughter Jazzy and I had the worst kind of flu at the same time. We spent the night together, comforting one another, suffering through it together. (I'll spare you the details.) But, at some point, she gave me one of the sweetest looks I've ever seen, and in a soft little weak voice she said, "Daddy, I'll never forget this. Thank you for being with me." She will never forget that experience, and neither will I. It was absolutely worth having to go through the worst flu of my life to hear those words.

To me, this is one of the most important points in this book. It's tempting to spend your life hoping it's going to be better later. Most of us look forward to promotions, special events, vacations, and highlights. And certainly these are wonderful things to anticipate. Yet, if we focus too much on these somewhat rare instances, we can miss out on the ordinary, yet incredibly special, events that happen on a regular basis—the beautiful smiles and laughter of children, the witnessing of simple acts of kindness, sharing a beautiful sunrise or sunset with someone you love, or witnessing the changing colors of the trees in the fall. These are the things life and memories are made of.

If you remind yourself to look for and appreciate the little things, your power of observation will be heightened. You'll begin to see "ordinary" experiences in a far more extraordinary manner. If you take a few moments to reflect on what truly matters in your life, I think you'll agree—in the end, it's the little things that matter most.

Surrender to the Fact That There's Always Something to Do

Sometimes making peace with the obvious is enormously helpful in preventing you from becoming overwhelmed or resentful. There are many observations about life that fall into this category, including: There's never enough time to get everything done; someone always has something you don't; you can't be in two places at the same time; there are trade-offs in life; tax day is April 15; you are going to get older and eventually die; you can't be all things to all people; and, of course, there's always something that needs to be done around the home!

For some reason, perhaps because these obvious things are so close to us, many of us tend to struggle against them. It's very common to hear people saying things like "My house is never the way I like it" or "No matter how hard I work, I can't get everything done." I have found it to be incredibly useful to surrender to certain aspects of life that are absolutely predictable. Near the top of this list is the fact that, regardless of where you live, who you are, or how much money you have or don't have, there's *always* something to do. No amount of complaining, simplifying, wishing it were different, or clever planning is going to change this simple fact of life. I have discovered that the best way to deal with this issue is to surrender to the fact that it's always going to be this way. I've known a number of people with virtually no money, a handful of people with all the money they could possibly need, and a huge number of people who fall somewhere in between. And no one, not a single person, has ever been exempt from this rule of life.

A few weeks ago, Kris and I spent a Saturday around the house trying to catch up on a few of our unfinished projects. As I looked around, I was shocked at how much we had to do. There was laundry to be done, floors to be washed, closets to be cleaned, and an attic that needed to be organized. My upstairs office looked as if I hadn't opened my mail in months, despite having sorted through it just the day before. The hamster cages needed to be cleaned, and the front porch was in need of sweeping. Of course, the kids' rooms required their daily attention, and our own bed needed to be made. The dog needed to be taken on a walk, and my younger daughter's bike seat needed to be raised. On top of all of this, the plants, both indoor and outdoor, needed watering.

Obviously, this was the mere tip of the iceberg. This simple list doesn't include the basic day-to-day stuff of life like paying the bills or reading to and spending time with the kids. Nor does it take into consideration the fact that the kids eat three meals a day, which take preparation and cleanup time. It also doesn't include major mainte-nance items, such as the fact that our home needs painting, or that there are many things such as appliances and garden furniture that are worn out and need to be fixed or replaced. It also doesn't account for the lawn that needs to be mowed each week and the rest of the garden that has accumulating weeds. I could go on, but I know you've got the picture!

When you step back for a moment, you can probably see how easy it can be to become discouraged (if not driven crazy) by all there is to do. If you decide you won't rest until everything is done, you will spend your entire lifetime very tired and frustrated. It's easy to sweat the small stuff at home because there is so much small stuff to contend with! The only way around this problem is to surrender, let go. Make the decision that it's okay to do your best even though it's a battle that, ultimately, can't be won. The best you can hope to do is stay on top of things, prioritize what's truly important, and maintain a sense of humor. In short, you can only do what you can do. Coming to the realization that inherent in life is the fact that you'll never be able to get everything done is not a defeatist attitude. It's simply an acknowledgment of the truth. The very fact that you're doing one thing suggests you aren't doing something else. So, starting today, give yourself a break. Relax. Do what you can but don't beat yourself up. You'll be much happier as a result.

71

Treat Your Family Members as if This Were the Last Time You Were Going to See Them

It's always difficult to know how to end a book. In *Don't Sweat the Small Stuff*, I concluded by suggesting that you live as if today were your last day on earth—because it might be; you never really know. I decided to bring this book to its conclusion by making a similar suggestion, only this time geared toward your family. In this strategy, I suggest that you treat your family members (and those you love most) as if this were the last time you were going to see them.

How often do we run out the door without saying good-bye—or say something less than kind or something critical under our breath as a parting shot as we go our separate ways? How often do we take for granted those we love and count on the most, assuming we will *always* be together? Most of us seem to operate under the assumption that we can always be kind later, that there's always tomorrow. But is that a wise way to live?

A few years ago, my grandmother Emily passed away. I remember visiting her, knowing that each visit might very well be the last time I ever saw her. Each visit counted and was treated as special. Each good-bye was filled with genuine love, appreciation, and reflection. Looking back, it was a particularly loving time because each moment was precious.

Our daily lives can be this precious. A powerful exercise to practice on a regular basis is to imagine that this is your final good-bye. Imagine that, for one reason or another, you won't see your family member ever again after this meeting. If this were true (and it's always a possibility), would you think and act in the same way? Would you remind your parent, child, sibling, spouse, or other loved one of yet another shortcoming, flaw, or imperfection in his or her behavior or personality? Would your last words be complaints or pessimistic comments that suggest that you wish your life were different than it is?

Probably not.

Perhaps, if you thought there was always the possibility that this was the last time you were going to see someone you love, you'd take an extra minute to give a loving hug and say good-bye. Or maybe you'd say something kind and gentle, an affirmation of your love, instead of your business-as-usual "See you later." If you thought this was the last time you were going to see your teenager, sister, parent, in-law, or spouse, you might treat that person differently, with more kindness, and more compassionately. Rather than rushing away, you'd probably smile and tell the person how much you care. Your heart would be open.

I make this suggestion not to create a fearful environment but to encourage you to remember how precious your family is and how much you'd miss them if they (or you) weren't around to share your life with. The implementation of this strategy into my life has added additional perspective to what's most important. I believe it can help you to become more patient and loving—and perhaps most of all, to remember to not sweat the small stuff with your family.

~≫ FROM ≪~

DON'T SWEAT THE SMALL STUFF FOR WOMEN

BY KRISTINE CARLSON

72

Wish Wonder Woman Good-bye

BY KRISTINE CARLSON

I saw a bumper sticker that said: "I am Woman. I am invincible. I am tired." Girlfriend, doesn't that say it all? Where do we women get the idea that we have to be perfect and do everything with the gusto and grace of Wonder Woman? There's no harm in giving everything you do the best you have to offer, but when your expectations are too high and your head hurts or your hair feels as though it could fall out, you need to consider wishing the Wonder Woman in you good-bye.

The key to this strategy is threefold. One, let go of the notion that you can do it all. When you can't accomplish everything on your list, that doesn't mean you're inadequate. Two, be willing to ask for help when you need it. Three, be willing to make changes when your system fails. If you can do these three things, you have begun to say good-bye to Wonder Woman!

I remember thinking that I would be the kind of woman who could easily balance motherhood, career, and outside interests, as well as have a perfect marriage. I did a pretty good job until our second daughter, our lovely Kenna, came along. Then my system failed and became out of balance. Kenna was one of the sweetest babies ever created. She was, however, an ear infection infant, and ran high fevers often. Dosed with antibiotics, she was sick a great deal of the time. Day care was out of the question; I wouldn't dream of having someone else care for my sick child. But Richard and I were running out of answers.

Finally, a solution came to me one stressed-out morning. As I finally quieted down, I realized that I was trying to maintain an image that was now totally out of control, and that was bigger than I had energy for or that I ever imagined it would be. It was as if a lightbulb went on; it became obvious that it was time to wish Wonder Woman good-bye—and that's exactly what I did!

I began to think it was time for my first career change; I was going to go from graphic designer to home manager. Although it wasn't the best of times financially, we decided that our family would be better served if I took a leave of absence from my business. I knew that this was probaby going to close a chapter in my personal history, and it wasn't going to be easy, as change rarely is. However, I decided that I needed to prioritize my family's needs (and sanity) over my own need to hold on to the "Wonder Woman" who thought she could handle running a business during nap times. It was just too much!

After the initial adjustment, I figured out that taking care of our two daughters full-time was a lot of fun, even if it meant less money—and it was so much more gratifying without the frustration of having a work schedule to attend to.

Stress is a very real phenomenon, but consider how much of it you create for yourself. If your husband's income alone is not enough to adequately provide for your family, then your only choice may be to go to work. On the other hand, if your husband's income is ample, yet you choose to work, and you're constantly stressed-out and made miserable by your job—well, in my book, that's a different story.

It might sound as if I'm making the case that all mothers should stay home with their children instead of working. I'm not. All I'm saying is that all of us need to take a look at our lives as circumstances change, and reflect on our priorities. As big events occur—bringing babies home from the hospital, having ill parents, or tending a sick child, for instance—we can't just expect our lives to go on as usual. We need to evaluate whether or not our current lifestyle best serves us, and if not, to navigate our way in a new direction by making small shifts and adjustments. Being stressed-out to the max virtually all the time is not giving your family the best you have to offer, because there's no way the material things you provide will replace your sanity, and that of your family.

If, on the other hand, you can create some flexibililty in your work schedule when needed, and you have excellent help, and all the family members are thriving, good for you—you've found a balance that works.

Keep in mind that Wonder Woman thinks she can do everything and be all things to everyone, all at once! She never says, "No, but thanks for asking," when asked to volunteer her time. She can't set limits, and she continues to add more and more to her calendar without letting go of anything. She darts here and there, leaving a frenetic trail of busyness. She adds one more committee to her list, or one more pet. She never says no to a lunch date or social request—unless, of course, she's already booked. She always takes in houseguests. Does she have a family? Well, if not, you can bet she plans on squeezing one into her schedule! Whatever her reasons, she does too much and eventually she caves in from exhaustion!

If this sounds familiar, it's time to reevaluate your "Wonder Woman" image and self-imposed expectations. Whether you're a stay-at-home, full-time mom or corporate executive; single, married with children, or otherwise; you need to ask yourself some basic questions. Would you enjoy your children more and have more to offer them emotionally if you took an occasional break? Are you spending too much time away from them in the name of good works? Is your home-based business totally taking over your life? How much of you does the company you work for really own, and how much are you willing to give up to continue to climb the corporate ladder?

The point is, if you're stressed, working too hard, and completely out of steam, consider what things you have control over and make some changes. Most important, realize that you don't have to be perfect—and that Wonder Woman is merely a figment of someone else's imagination.

Cut Your Friends Some Slack

BY KRISTINE CARLSON

Aren't there days when you just want to say what's on your mind without anyone questioning you? Or misquote a fact and not be corrected? Perhaps you're not feeling well, and the last thing you want from a good friend is for her to take your mood personally or attempt to talk you out of the way you're feeling. Wouldn't it be nice if you could make a mistake, or say the wrong thing, or mess up, or be too critical, and have your friends just let it slide? It sure would be nice if we could count on our friends to cut us some slack, from time to time, and we should surely do the same for them.

Suppose your friend calls you, and you can tell by her tone of voice that she's having a bad day. Maybe she's on the verge of tears, or maybe she's just stressed out. As much as you want to say it, this is clearly not the time to remind her to "not be late" (as she was the last two times) on her carpool turn to pick up the kids for soccer. Neither is it the time to be critical of her, question her, or to stir things up in some way. Now's not the time to bring up an issue, suggest she's seeing things wrong, or make any concrete suggestions. It's certainly not a good idea to launch into your own story of misery, or to complain about your life.

Instead, this is a day to cut her some slack. Let her be human.

Give her a break. Even if her low mood encourages her to say something you don't like—so what, just let it go! In fact, if you are a really good friend, you might even consider changing your schedule around and driving for her that afternoon. It might be just the right breathing room she needs to get her bearings back. If you can be this kind of friend, you'll be loved forever!

Friendships, especially with your girlfriends, are to be cherished. Who is it who helps you out with the kids when you've got the flu and your husband has to be at work? Who is it you turn to when you're feeling low and you need a shoulder to lean on or cry on? Who is it that picks you up when your marriage fails or some catastrophe happens? These are some of the reasons to cut your friends some slack, and not hold them to impossible expectations and standards, especially when they are having a bad day.

Sometimes, we get so close to our friends that it's easy to forget that they are just human—like we are. They're going to get in low moods, make mistakes, say the wrong thing, be overly critical, use poor judgment, disagree with some of your opinions, and so forth. Everyone, even our friends, can be insensitive at times, quick-tempered, in need of space, or feel like they're going crazy! The best friends in the world are those who remember this—those who accept this—those who love their friends in spite of it all. The best friends are those who cut their friends some slack, those who make allowances for their friends' imperfections.

Most of all, remember that if you have a live-in housemate, husband, boyfriend, or life partner, don't forget that they are your "best friends," and go ahead and cut them some slack too! Often the people we live with don't get the best of us, but instead the worst! Cutting each other some slack will do wonders to your long-range happiness as a couple.

In the long run, cutting your friends some slack will greatly reduce your own stress. You'll feel good about yourself, knowing that you allow people to be fully human, even though they are far from perfect. You'll also be loved, cherished, and appreciated for being willing to love your friends just the way they are.

74

Perhaps It's Not Personal

BY KRISTINE CARLSON

If there's one thing that many women have in common, it's our sensitive natures. Along with this quality comes a tendency to internalize and impute meaning and motive to the behavior and actions of others. Here's a thought: Rather than going with your immediate reaction, consider that, at least some of the time, the things that happen really have nothing to do with you, personally, at all. It just may be that you are trusting the erroneous thoughts and feelings that have warped your perception, rather than admitting to yourself that perhaps it's not personal. Let me give you a few scenarios that might seem familiar.

You have an acquaintance that you've met in school through your kids. Every time you see her, she doesn't even acknowledge you. In fact, she seems to look right past you. You begin to feel uncomfortable, thinking, "What's her problem, anyway?" You start to get mad, as she obviously thinks she's too good for you. But have you considered the possibilities that could easily explain her apparent standoffishness? Maybe she's nearsighted. Maybe she doesn't make eye contact because she doesn't have time to socialize. Maybe she has other things on her mind. Maybe she's thinking the same thing about you. Just maybe, it's not personal.

Your spouse gets home and is in a low mood. He's been putting out fires all day. You've put out a few of your own today, as well, and you were looking forward to an enthusiastic reception. Instead, he retreats to his office, grumbling that he's not hungry for dinner, he has too much work still to do. Need I say more? Rather than blow up and have a nasty confrontation, consider that perhaps it's not personal. He's simply had a bad day.

Taking things personally only causes you unnecessary frustration, while leaving other people baffled by your reactions. We've temporarily attached our self-worth to another person's apparent actions and motives.

It's helpful to step back and see the bigger picture. We need to have a bit more self-preservation and higher self-esteem than that. We need to break the habit of overreacting because of our speedy assumptions and judgments. So the next time you catch yourself annoyed at a person or situation, remember to say to yourself: "Perhaps it's not personal—and so what if it is!"

75

Let Go of Your "Perfect" Plans

BY KRISTINE CARLSON

You decide to have a party to celebrate your father's sixtieth birthday, or your parents' golden fiftieth wedding anniversary, or perhaps you're planning a neighborhood barbecue. Or, maybe you just want to get away for a romantic weekend.

Whatever the occasion, you embark upon your planning with pure determination that it will be "the perfect day" and you will have the "perfect party."

Unfortunately, as you've undoubtedly already experienced, these "expectations" are surefire, 100 percent guaranteed to at best ensure your disappointment; at median to be a highly stressful experience; and at worst, to give you the beginning of an ulcer.

If you would like to ensure a great party where you also end up enjoying the whole experience, remember to do your best in planning the details, but at the same time, let go of your "perfect" plans. Make allowances, up front, for the fact that there are twists and "speed bumps" in all plans. No matter how attentive you are to details and regardless of your ability to anticipate problems, there's always going to be something you didn't plan. Knowing this in advance is a tremendous source of stress prevention.

We place a tremendous amount of unnecessary pressure on ourselves by having too-high expectations. If you're a perfectionist, this strategy will apply to you doubly. It's helpful to come to peace with the fact that there are too many variables that are out of your control whenever you plan an event. I have yet to hear of a person who can control the weather, how much Uncle Jim drinks that night, or some of the weird family dynamics that are all but certain to occur.

A good indication that your expectations may be running a little high lies in how you are treating your family, caterer, and friends right before the big event. If you are short-tempered, flustered, and snappy, and your face breaks out, chances are, it's time to throw your hands in the air and remember that the party will go on even if you're stressed out! Take a moment to breathe and to lighten up. Try to remember that your initial motivation for planning this occasion came from the inspiration to celebrate and have some fun.

Here's another scenario that never seems to fail: you plan an incredibly romantic weekend away with your husband, forgetting to plan around the one thing that can truly botch it up in a big way. Then, bingo! The day you leave, you get your period. This has happened to me several times. It can be a bummer, but if you can keep your sense of humor and be a little flexible, you can always manage to have a great time anyway.

When something like this happens to us, we simply let go of our original "perfect plan" and go for "Plan B," which includes backrubs, footrubs, long intimate walks on the beach, or in the woods. Deep conversation and candlelit baths become the focus of the weekend. The only time we've failed to have a good time together is when one or the other of us gets too uptight about our "perfect plan."

On a grander life scale, the same strategy applies. If you think you can map out the perfect life and expect that all will stick to your plan, well, good luck. Some things will turn out as you desired, while others will not. We rarely plan to get ill, or fired, or to have to move suddenly for a job.

Often we plan around our expectations of what marriage will be like, or what it will be like once a baby is born. Some of it will turn out as we thought, while much of it will be different from our expectations. The question is how invested you are in the idea that things have to turn out according to your plan. The more invested in your expectations, the more disappointment you will feel when those expectations don't turn out as planned.

One way to look at it is this: Instead of being upset when things don't go according to plans, be pleasantly surprised when, once in awhile, something you plan actually meets your expectations! Then, you'll be able to enjoy an event, either way. You'll know that things will be "perfect" just the way they are!

76

Don't Be a Backseat Driver

BY KRISTINE CARLSON

There are few things more irritating than having someone sit in the backseat of your car, firing off instructions while you're driving. Unless the advice is really needed, as in the case of an emergency or something the driver truly doesn't notice, backseat driving is virtually always unasked for.

Interestingly enough, the same can be said about what you might call "backseat living," meaning someone who is trying to live someone else's life for them or someone who is living their life vicariously through someone else. The classic example of this dynamic is a parent who always wanted to be a great athlete or musician, but wasn't able to make it happen for themselves. So now, as a parent, they push their kids to become accomplished in one of those fields, and they take their pushing to an extreme. Their self-worth is tied up in how well the kids do or don't do.

Backseat living is highly stressful. Not only do you push away and ultimately alienate the people whose lives you are trying to influence, but you also feel incredible amounts of stress and disappointment over things you have no control over. It's hard enough keeping your cool when your own tennis game needs work, but impossible to keep your emotions in check if your sense of well-being is tied to whether your son or daughter happens to win the tournament or whether your boyfriend has the ambition you think he should have!

Being supportive and enthusiastic, of course, are entirely different subjects. I'm referring here to crossing the line into truly unhealthy territory, in which the other person feels pushed and not accepted, and you feel stressed out!

The key to breaking this habit is to first have the humility to admit to yourself that, at times, you practice backseat living. By identifying yourself in that role, you'll be able to take a step back and see the bigger picture. Once you see yourself as a backseat driver (so to speak), the rest is easy—simply turn the tables. Imagine what it would be like to have someone trying to drive your life, always looking over your shoulder, offering unsolicited advice, judging your actions, acting disappointed and disapproving, and so forth. Once you imagine this happening to you, it's pretty easy to see how distasteful it can be. Then you can learn to increase your compassion and back off.

One of the greatest gifts you can offer someone you love is to let them know, in no uncertain terms, that you love them and approve of them, exactly as they are. They don't need to change, or be any different, or take your advice—you simply love them. It's comforting to know that there are people in our lives who have confidence in us, people who show us through their actions that they believe in, and have faith in us.

Life is such a magical gift to be treasured. Perhaps we should allow others to experience this gift without the burden of our backseat driving. To let go of this habit is a gift to those we love, as well as to ourselves.

77

Go Ahead and Vent (One Time), But Get It Off Your Chest

BY KRISTINE CARLSON

I don't know about you, but when I'm really bugged about something, it's my tendency to vent it—not once, but many times. I'll repeat the same story over and over again. I've even found myself telling one friend—and then another, and another—until I run out of friends to tell! Then I might start again with friend number one, until she gently reminds me that I've told her the story already. Venting becomes a sort of sport, something we do to entertain ourselves, to pass time, and to convince ourselves that we are justified in being annoyed by whatever is bothering us.

It has become clear to me, however, by observing my own feelings and those of others, that such "repeat venting" destroys any potentially positive aspects of the process. Whereas one venting session can be useful, even healing, repetition only bogs you down and stresses you out. Repeat venting serves to feed our hamster wheel mode of thinking, and instead of feeling any sense of relief, we create even more anger and frustration by keeping our stressful thoughts alive. The things that bother us are fed by our attention to them; venting is the perfect way to "stuff" ourselves with our troubles.

Just as we wouldn't intentionally rub salt into an open abscess, if we absolutely must vent (which should be done only to try to gain insight), try doing it with one person, one time, and let it go after that.

There's no question that venting can adversely affect your marriage. Talking about the things that bother you once is fine, but to do so over and over again simply keeps you bothered, and keeps your attention on what is wrong in your life. I've learned that repeated venting is a clear sign that I'm in a low mood, and commiseration with someone else who is also feeling down will surely take you even lower! The most effective way to feel better isn't even more venting, but instead it is to drop these issues and let them rest awhile. Be assured that they will still be there tomorrow if they are real issues, only you'll feel better and will be able to handle them a bit more reasonably.

Go ahead and give yourself permission, one time, to vent to someone else. Get it off your chest, and feel good about doing so. However, try to catch yourself when you go too far. See if you can resist the temptation to stay stuck in negative feelings, which is precisely what happens when you repeatedly vent the same thoughts. I'm guessing that you'll feel a profound difference the very first time you catch yourself and avoid the temptation. Good luck.

78

Rise Above the Rut of Your Routine

BY KRISTINE CARLSON

Bake bread on Monday. Marketing on Tuesday. Laundry on Wednesday . . . etc. Many people find a routine comforting, as it gives them some feelings of control in life. What can sneak up on us and catch us unaware, however, is an emotional rut that leaves us feeling empty and uninspired. If you are having these feelings, consider finding a time either weekly or daily to expand your horizons a bit and make a minor shift in your routine. A fresher outlook will help you to rise above your rut and the feelings that go with it.

The first step in rising above the rut of your routine is to spend some quiet time reflecting and dreaming a bit. Notice what pops up in your head: it may be something you've been longing to do, but simply have continued to put off. This is the first baby step in learning to live from the source of your inspiration as opposed to staying in the gridlock of your routine.

Some people are a bit structure-stiff. They never deviate from their day-to-day routine, which makes them feel safe. These people can lack fresh inspiration, look more tired and older every year, and never appear to feel enriched or excited about living. While there are certainly parts of our routines such as school schedules, athletic practices, and work schedules that are rarely negotiable, you can sometimes find some small chunks of time that may be.

Consider learning a new language; dare to dream of visiting that country and getting to know the people there. Take an art class. Join a book club, or better yet, start one. Join a church, temple, or other spiritual center. Take up yoga. Alter your exercise routine. There are hundreds of possibilities.

It also does wonders to try to make spontaneous plans, at least every once in a while. I know this becomes more difficult once you have a family with schedules to plan around, but go ahead and find a negotiable slot in your week and do something different. It might be as simple as forgoing the kids' normal homework time for a family nature walk instead. Or, call some neighbors on Sunday morning and invite them over for a barbecue that evening. Give yourself the joy of doing something unplanned or different. It can shake you up and inspire a fresh perspective on life.

Another way to make a simple shift in your routine is by altering your normal driving routes. You might take the more scenic back roads home from work now and then, instead of always getting on the freeway. Driving can be a pleasure if you're not always on the same routes. Also, as you alter your route, consider that it may even be safer for you and your family as it may keep you more attentive and alert. Taking the same route all the time tends to make us daydream.

It is amazing how making one slight shift, in what seems an insignificant gesture, can inspire and uplift your spirit. This feeling will spill over into other areas of your life as you send your unconscious mind the message that you are open to new possibilities. It also, very simply stated, makes life a little less bland and a lot more original.

79

Say "No, but Thanks for Asking" (Without Feeling Guilty)

BY KRISTINE CARLSON

Here's an important strategy for all women who do too much! When you've hit your limit on how much you can do, and do with joy, it's imperative to your well-being to learn to say, "No, but thanks for asking." And it's important to learn to say these words without feeling any sense of guilt whatsoever.

Before you can apply this strategy, however, you'll probably want to evaluate, and come to terms with, exactly what your limits are: what you're able to do, what you're willing to do, and what you want to do.

The problem with taking on more committees, responsibilities, and leadership activities than you really have time for, is that eventually you will hit your limit—very suddenly—in the form of burnout and resentment.

All of a sudden, you'll have so much going on that you won't know how to turn back. You'll feel exhausted and overwhelmed, perhaps even resentful and bitter because too much has once again fallen into your lap. Your failure to say "No" without feeling guilty will have created a nightmare for yourself.

When you belong to an organization, of course you need to do your part. However, you can pick and choose based on what's going on in your life and the number of commitments you already have. You need to give yourself permission to say that enough is enough.

When you begin to acknowlege all that you do accomplish, your guilt will subside. There is tremendous power in knowing that you aren't buried with burdens your heart isn't really into. A clearer mind and a slightly more manageable schedule allows you to make decisions from a place of clarity rather than from a place of frantic desperation.

As you learn to say no without guilt, the events in which you do play a leadership role will give you greater joy and gratification. Not to mention that as you stop overextending yourself, you will do a finer job on those things in which you choose to participate.

Once you decide to decline the offer, it's best to do so without offering a litany of reasons why you can't. (That's a clue that you're feeling guilty.) Have you ever noticed that you lose the person's attention once you launch into the "why." People aren't interested in your busyness—they're contending with too much busyness of their own.

"People pleasers" find it most difficult to say no. They want to be liked so badly, they'll gladly sacrifice their own well-being. However, if you have to back out at the last minute because of other commitments, you aren't going to be liked very much. It's better not to commit in the first place than to leave someone in the lurch!

Learning to say "no" to your work, whether you own your own business or are an employee, is important, too. Remember that if you work long past 5:30 every night, you're cutting short your time with your husband and/or your children. Again, it's a question of balance. A good way to think of it is: Refuse to work those hours you aren't being paid for (i.e., late evenings and weekends).

You may also be tempted by your guilt to over-commit your social calendar. However, you'd better be on the same page as your spouse, boyfriend, or significant other, or your guilty "yesses" could cause you more frustration than you bargained for. Your partner may have a completely different social agenda and set of priorities. They may not appreciate doing things simply because you feel guilty!

Keep in mind that you may not be wasting only your own time by making commitments based on guilt, but also that of the people you say yes to. After all, would they really want to spend time with people who are only with them out of obligation and guilt?

So, the next time someone asks you if you'd like to chair a committee, organize a fundraiser, go on a field trip, work in a classroom, or even go out to dinner, take a moment to reflect. Honestly contemplate whether you really have the desire and the spare time before giving them an answer. If you feel as if you're overextended, or the timing is simply off, simply say, "No, but thanks for asking," and leave it at that.

80

Be 99 Percent Gossip-Free

BY KRISTINE CARLSON

I considered calling this chapter "No More Gossip for Sport," but I don't like to advocate "doing as I say and not as I do." I realized that I'd be digging myself a hole I couldn't get out of, as it seems that nearly everyone—and I am no exception—partakes of gossip in one form or another. Try as I might to limit what I say about other people to other people, I realize that I'm more likely to have success in this area (and you might too) if the standard is to be 99 percent gossip-free.

The study of human behavior is far too interesting, it seems, to keep our observations and hearsay to ourselves! When we're really honest with ourselves, don't you think we find a sense of safety and relief in sharing something juicy that's happening to someone else? We're grateful, as our mouths are saying the words, that it's them and not us. It also seems that we're more prone to gossip about people we aren't that fond of, or perhaps are a bit envious of, for one reason or another (and this probably isn't something we'd be willing to admit).

Our need for gossip could stem from a bit of boredom with what's happening—or not happening—in our own lives. We may attempt to appear more interesting to someone we're talking to by having the "hottest" news.

I had a college roommate who left a dramatic impression on me. We used to spend long hours talking about everything from boys to the spiritual side of life. Occasionally, as someone's name would come up, I would begin to make an observation about this person. She would stop me dead in my tracks, put her hands over her ears, and proclaim: "I won't speak or hear anything about another person that is mean or potentially not true!" This would crack me up, and truthfully, there were times when, just to check her consistency, I would test her on purpose. But to no avail—she was committed 100 percent to this rule! I had nothing but the greatest admiration for her. She set such a great example, and I knew I could trust her with any secret.

Unless you want to be known for being a gossip who will say anything to anyone, try to limit your gossip to one friend, as I do, and even then, don't indulge in it too often. Be 99 percent gossip-free, and whatever you say, don't ever gossip about the one friend you gossip to!

81

Treasure the Journey

BY KRISTINE CARLSON

Ah . . . what a concept: Treasure the journey. Before your mind skips to the trials and tribulations that you may face today, or the fact that today your life might not be what you had expected or hoped for, take the time to repeat these words to yourself: Today, I will treasure the journey.

To "treasure" something means to hold it close to your heart. When we talk about treasuring the journey, what I mean is that we hold the gift of life itself with the highest regard; to make it an adventure marked by your personal path of discovery.

Richard often says in his lectures, "Life is a process, not a destination." It's not like you're going to "get somewhere" and all will be well. Instead, the joy is in the path itself. Your journey is the day-to-day, moment-to-moment process, and the attitude that you bring to that path has everything to do with what you will receive along the way. The question is this: Do you anticipate what life is going to be like someday, or do you live life as it unfolds right now? Your answer will determine whether your life is experienced as an adventure, or whether it's constantly on hold until further notice!

I'll admit that there are days when we wake up and it feels more like we will be trudging through a muddy trail, with poison oak on all sides, than skipping freely through a meadow of wildflowers with the wind in our hair. It's precisely on these heavier days that we must remember to treasure the journey.

It's helpful to remind ourselves that on every great vacation we've ever been on, at least one thing went wrong, yet we refused to let it ruin our good time. It's with this same spirit that we must embark upon each day as a new beginning that holds an adventure in the wings of each moment. (Some of which, admittedly, we'd rather not go through again.)

I was once sitting in a café in Berkeley in a reflective state of mind. I watched all the people walking by for several minutes. With each person's appearance screaming "individuality" as it does in Berkeley, I thought to myself how grand it is that there are as many different people as shapes and colors. I was acutely aware that each person who walked by had a unique story to tell, complete with a past, present, and future.

The culmination of our experiences completes our own unique biography; every person makes their mark in history with their own story to tell, and each day represents the turning of the page. From the time you wake until the time you go to sleep at night, you mark your journey in fleeting moments and passing days. As you make it your single-minded intention to treasure this journey you are on, you begin to feel great gratitude as well as great love. You see that life gives you all of what you need, and some of what you ask for. Every event has purpose and meaning, and you know that "the small stuff" doesn't really mean much at all. In fact, it's fretting and worrying and dwelling on the small stuff that keeps you from treasuring your experiences daily.

As women, we have the world at our fingertips, with everything within our reach for the first time in history. All we have to do is spread our wings, navigate our direction with some good common sense and a lot of heart and soul, and fly like the wind.

So, make it a habit to wake up each day with the intention to see life as an incredible adventure—a journey to be treasured. Life is a great gift; it is the treasure at the end of the rainbow. As you begin each day, keeping this in mind, you'll experience wonder and awe as you open yourself to bliss.

As I close, I'd like to thank you for reading this section and sharing this treasured part of my journey.

With heartfelt affection
in love and light,
Kris

DON'T SWEAT THE SMALL STUFF IN LOVE

WITH KRISTINE CARLSON

82

Mostly, Be Pals

WITH KRISTINE CARLSON

I had to choose a single characteristic that has made our relationship remain special, fun, and vibrant over the years, it would probably be that the two of us are, first and foremost, really good pals. Make no mistake about it—we're all the other things too. We are committed to each other and faithful. We share an overwhelming love for our children, similar values and goals, many of the same friends, shared interests, and mutual respect, as well as an attraction for one another. We are also blessed with the same spiritual values and beliefs. Yet, as wonderful and important as all of these other characteristics are, none of them guarantees keeping your love for each other alive and strong.

After all, there are many faithful couples who bicker in the car on their way to church. There are plenty of wonderful and dedicated parents who share similar values. Yet, they are constantly irritated at one another. There are also tons of couples who have mutual friends, share similar hobbies and interests, and are physically attracted to each other, who nevertheless fight like crazy, experience jealousy, and just can't seem to get along for extended periods of time.

When you are good friends first, however, everything seems to take care of itself. Pals support one another. They are patient and kind, and make allowances for each other's imperfections. Friends are excellent communicators, and usually very good listeners. While they can also be serious, when appropriate, pals also find it easy to have fun, and to laugh. They stay connected, sharing in the good times and being there for each other during difficult times.

The best way to remain (or get back to being) pals is to see what's in it for you and for your relationship. Once you are convinced that having a great friendship is the best way to secure a great relationship, the rest is pretty easy. Keep reminding yourself that your goal is to treat your partner with the same kindness, appreciation, and respect as you would your very best friend in the world. When in doubt, ask yourself, "If this person were my best friend, how would I respond and how would I act?"

Many people say, "My partner *is* my best friend," but most don't actually back up that statement with thoughts, feelings, and actions consistent with it. To the contrary, many individuals treat their partner with more jealousy, expectations, and demands—and with less appreciation, respect, and sensitivity—than they would a friend. Many people treat their partner as if they own them, and seem more interested in the image of who they want their partner to be than in who their partner really is.

If a friend said to you, "My dream is to change careers. It will mean less money, but I know I'll be happier," or if she said, "My dream is to live near the ocean," you'd probably be enthused and supportive. But what if your partner said the same thing to you? How would you respond? Would you be supportive, take it to heart, and try to help her make it happen? Or would you automatically disregard it, or in some way minimize it—saying or thinking, "You can't (or shouldn't) do that. It's not practical. It's not what I want."

Obviously, the spirit of your answer is what's most important. It's not always possible, practical, or even desirable for your partner to do everything he or she wants to do. You can't always move or change jobs. We're not suggesting that it's necessary to always want what your partner wants, or that it's your responsibility to make it happen. Instead, we are saying that it's important to remember how friends treat friends and to take that into consideration in your relationship. What's most important is that your partner knows that you're genuinely supportive of her dreams, whether she can fulfill them or not.

We can assure you, firsthand, that being really good friends is a gift, and a goal worth pursuing. When you are good pals, you somehow find a way to meet in the middle, and to share in each other's dreams without feeling like you're sacrificing a thing. Implementing this strategy may take some reflection and the willingness to change a few habits, but it's well worth the effort.

83

Learn to Laugh at Yourself

WITH KRISTINE CARLSON

Almost nothing immunizes you from day-to-day frustration more than a healthy sense of humor—particularly the ability to laugh at yourself. Every long-term relationship gets to a point where your partner knows you almost as well as you know yourself. He will see your quirks, anticipate your unhealthy responses, and know the ways that you sometimes get in your own way. Even if you tried, it would be difficult to hide your true self from your partner.

If you are unable to laugh at yourself, you're in for a long, bumpy ride. You will struggle in your relationships because, as your partner teases you, notices your flaws, and occasionally points them out, you will feel and probably act a bit defensive. This, in turn, will exacerbate and highlight your weaknesses, making them seem far more significant. What's more, your reactions to your partner's comments will create additional issues for the two of you to deal with, and your "small stuff" will start to seem like big stuff.

If you look around at the happiest and most loving relationships, you'll almost always notice that both people have an ability to laugh at themselves. Both partners will have the perspective necessary to stay lighthearted as their own imperfections come to the surface. This creates an environment where occasional teasing or kidding around is okay, and where one feels safe in making observations or suggestions. Your relationship has the chance to deepen and grow because both parties feel safe.

It's quite remarkable to observe what happens to a potentially heated interaction when someone is able to keep their sense of humor. In most cases, the situation is diffused and simply melts away. For example, we were sharing time with another couple when the woman made a slightly snide comment to her husband. Specifically, she said, "You talk too much." His response speaks to the point of this strategy. He laughed to himself and said, very gently, "You're right, I sure can dominate a conversation." More than his words, his ability to see a grain of truth in his wife's statement, to remain humble, and to be willing to chuckle at his own tendency resolved the situation before it had a chance to gain any momentum. Often, when you keep your sense of humor and remain humble, your partner will sense when he has been too harsh and will end up apologizing for his comment. Even if this doesn't happen, it doesn't really matter because to you, it was no big deal to begin with.

Over the years, we've seen hundreds of similar conversations turn ugly because, instead of keeping a sense of humor and remaining lighthearted, the person on the receiving end of the not-so-nice comment became defensive and took himself too seriously. His inability to have a sense of humor encouraged him to lash back, argue, or start a fight.

When someone takes himself too seriously, you can sense it, even when he keeps his reactions to himself. His mood changes, as do his mannerisms, his tone of voice, and his body language. There are no two ways about it: Without a sense of humor, you end up suffering.

Remember that, as wonderful as you are, your partner spends a great deal of time with you. If your partner makes occasional observations that are less than sugar-coated, there may be a grain of truth in what she is saying. But even if your partner is off base entirely, it's probably in your best interest to simply let it go—laugh it off. By laughing at yourself, not taking yourself so seriously, you will become much easier to be around. Your partner won't feel as though she has to walk around on eggshells, making sure you don't get upset. And in the end, because you will have created a more nourishing and safe environment for your partner, your relationship will be more loving and a heck of a lot more fun.

84

Throw Away Your Scorecard

WITH KRISTINE CARLSON

If you wanted an absolutely predictable, completely reliable way to guarantee ongoing frustration—and a virtually guaranteed way to adversely affect your relationship—it would be to keep score of what you do, and of what your partner isn't doing. And if you really wanted to compound the problem, you could let your partner know, on a regular basis, how he or she isn't meeting your expectations—and how much more you are doing than he or she is!

As ludicrous as this idea may seem, it's precisely what many couples do, without knowing it, every day of their lives together. This habit contributes to resentment, frustration, apathy, and an overall breakdown of an otherwise positive relationship.

For various reasons, it's tempting to keep track, either silently or even out loud, of all that you're doing to contribute to the relationship, to make your partner's life easier, and how much you sacrifice in the name of the relationship. You think of how many times in a row you've cleaned the house, or paid the bills, or driven to work, or done the laundry, or bathed the children, or whatever.

Perhaps we do this for fear we won't be appreciated—or maybe it's because we're slightly resentful of the role we find ourselves in—or perhaps it's something altogether different. Whatever the reason, it backfires.

When you engage in this extremely common habit, two things are certain. First, your excessive thinking about the perceived inequities in your relationship will frustrate you and stress you out. When you constantly remind yourself of your own hard work, you'll invariably feel angry at your partner, and in many cases, your loving feelings will diminish. The connection between your thinking and the way you feel is undeniable. As you think about your resentments and fill your mind with your unfair task load, you'll feel the effects of those burdensome thoughts—you'll feel taken advantage of and burned out.

Second, your partner will feel your resentment and built-up tension—which will give him or her more negativity to latch on to and think about. No one wants to feel as though his or her partner is put off and angered by the contributions he or she is making. In fact, the usual response to discovering this is to become defensive about how much he or she is doing in comparison. Both parties dig in and think even more about how much they are doing—scorecards are flying! Negative feelings surround your relationship, and both partners think the other is to blame.

As your scorecard enters your mind, see if you can drop those thoughts and bring yourself back to a loving feeling. Remind yourself that it's easier to see your own contribution and to take your partner's efforts for granted. For the moment, reverse this thought process. Think not of what your partner isn't doing, but instead think of what he is doing. You may discover that some portion of your frustration isn't reality, but simply a mental habit that has crept into your thinking. Each time you dismiss your "this isn't fair" thinking, you'll be contributing to the good will of your relationship. In fact, Kris and I have discovered that, ultimately, keeping your scorecard thinking to a minimum actually contributes more to a loving relationship than any of the more concrete contributions you are making—the ones you are fretting about.

Even if your scorecard mentality persists, and you're absolutely convinced that you are getting the short end of the stick, it's still best that you keep your thinking in check. In doing so, you'll keep your loving feelings alive. Remember, it's always easier to have heartfelt discussions or discuss difficult issues when your heart is filled with love and patience. Admittedly, both Kris and I still occasionally fall into this trap, but luckily it's pretty rare. We think you'll find that if you can nip this tendency in the bud, the mutual love and respect in your relationship will return—or get even stronger.

85

Avoid the Words, "I Love You, But"

WITH KRISTINE CARLSON

There's no question that three of the most beautiful and longed-for words in any language are "I love you." Left alone, they can bring forth feelings of warmth and connection. However, you can virtually destroy the beauty as well as much of the positive impact of these wonderful words by doing nothing other than adding the word "but" to the end of the phrase. Doing so turns a statement of innocence and respect into a manipulative and self-serving lecture.

Kris was the first woman to teach me this important lesson. Years ago, shortly after we fell in love, she looked me in the eye and asked me the question, "Are you aware that you have qualified your love for me twice in the past five minutes?" At the time, I didn't even know what she meant. She went on to explain that while she appreciated the fact that I enjoyed telling her that I loved her, the truth was that my words seemed far less genuine when I attached a condition. Specifically, I had told her, "I love you, BUT I want you to stop keeping me waiting" and "I love you, BUT it bothers me when you assume I'll want to do something when your friends are involved." Later she told me that she was bringing it up because it was becoming a habit, and she hoped I could nip it in the bud.

When she first brought this to my attention, I was a little defensive. I've since learned, however, that there was no reason to be. Kris wasn't making a statement that she was above criticism, or that I wasn't free to bring up issues that were bugging me. To the contrary, she encouraged it (and still does). What she was asking me to do was to separate my "I love you's" from any issues I was having with her. She was correctly pointing out that while both ends of the spectrum (the expression of love and the freedom to discuss issues) are important in an honest, loving relationship, the two are absolutely unrelated.

As I thought about it, it made perfect sense. When you examine the intent of the word "but" after the words "I love you," it becomes clear that the only reason you would connect the two would be to make your gripe or complaint appear more reasonable. Rather than having the courage to simply bring up the issues that were concerning me, I was making certain that, first, I looked like a good guy. In a way it was like saying, "I'm a really nice, patient, and tolerant guy who really loves you. And now that we've established all of this, let me tell you how I want you to change so that you will be even more loving in my eyes."

If that isn't grotesque, what is? It has "hidden agenda" written all over it!

Since that time, I've heard this "add-on" hundreds, maybe even thousands, of times. Often, as was the case with me, it's delivered directly from one person to his partner. In many other instances it's delivered secondhand. For example, just yesterday I was talking to a woman on the phone who told me, "I really love Kurt, BUT I can't stand it when he interrupts me."

This is a very simple idea that pays enormous dividends. The idea, as Kris originally taught me, is to avoid connecting your loving praise with the things that are bothering you. When you feel love for your partner, tell her. Likewise, when something bothers you, share that too. Just don't do it at the same time. If you're at all like me, you'll soon discover that both your compliments and your concerns will be taken far more seriously.

86

Remember That Your Partner Can't Read Your Mind

WITH KRISTINE CARLSON

It seems to us that one of the worst mistakes many of us make in our relationships is that, without even knowing it, we assume, at times, that our partner can read our mind. Or, if we don't assume she can do so, we very often expect her to.

I was talking to a friend when he started to complain of his wife's inability to stay organized. He seemed tormented by the issue and, in fact, he had brought this subject to my attention on several previous occasions. Finally, I asked him, "Does Carol know how much this bugs you?" It turned out that she had no idea that it concerned him in the least!

There are several good reasons why it's important to recognize this problem, and to nip it in the bud. First, and most obviously, it creates a great deal of grief and inner turmoil for yourself. You carry around a ton of frustration that has little, if anything, to do with you. You're mad, bothered, or irritated about something—and you're the only one who knows about it. If that isn't self-induced stress, what is?

Second, it's not really fair to your partner. Here you are steaming mad about something, and you don't even give your partner the courtesy of telling her what it is that's bugging you. You're probably coming across as mad or irritated, but she doesn't even know what it's about. In cases like these, you're demanding that she read your mind! What chance does she have? How can she explain herself, much less do anything about it?

The first thing that bothered me about Kris was her tendency to keep me waiting. After a while I started fuming about it. I told my good friends; I sulked, complained, and wished she would change. Finally, when I couldn't stand it any longer, I brought it up to her. In a very sincere, nondefensive tone, she said, "I'm really sorry. I didn't even realize I was doing it. I wish you would have told me sooner." It turned out that while I was obsessively punctual, she was quite comfortable running a few minutes behind schedule. She simply didn't think that it was a big deal and had no idea it was bothering me. So, while keeping people waiting may not be a great idea, clearly the responsibility of dealing with the issue was in my hands. I was expecting Kris to read my mind. And while she has many magical qualities, reading my mind is not one of them.

What we've learned is that, when something is bothering you, it's usually best to let your partner know about it. Pick a time when neither of you is in a defensive mood. Then bring up the issue gently and respectfully and see what happens. It seems logical that, in most cases, your chances of a favorable outcome are far better than if you rely on your partner reading your mind. If at all possible, avoid the self-destructive thought, "He (or she) should know what I want or need." You'll make it easier on yourself and on your relationship if you go ahead and let your partner know.

87

Don't Fight Over Stupid Things

WITH KRISTINE CARLSON

This strategy speaks right to the heart of the matter. Fighting over stupid things is another way of saying you're sweating the small stuff—big time! Yet, we see it all the time: couples arguing and bickering over the most ridiculous things. People argue over who misplaced the scissors, whose turn it is to take out the trash, which one of you has more free time, who works harder, or whether or not you had fun at last year's family reunion! People argue over who is a better driver or a more dedicated parent, or who came in second place in a contest that took place last year. People get furious over having to wait a few minutes when their partner is running a little late, when their table manners fall short of perfection, or when their partner misinterprets a fact. We even know a woman who started a fight because her husband put the towels in the wrong bathroom! Wow. What could possibly be more significant than that?

Ironically, many couples will tell you that they rarely bicker over truly significant issues. So it seems to make sense that if one or both persons in a relationship could eliminate all fights (give or take a few) over stupid things, all would be well—at least most of the time.

When you eliminate (or even greatly reduce) the number of little things that bother you enough to fight about, it opens the door to a different kind of relationship. It's so much fun to be around someone who isn't always bothered by something—it's refreshing, inviting, and nourishing. When you refuse to fight over stupid things, you can become true pals again—partners in every sense of the word.

When things don't get to you so much, when your patience and perspective are intact, you reinforce (or remind) your partner why he or she is so fond of you—your sense of humor begins to come out, you become more interesting and introspective, and you're just plain more fun to be around.

Both of us have always made the assumption that a good relationship is something people crave for many reasons—not the least of which is that when you're with someone who isn't easily bothered, who doesn't sweat the small stuff in love, it's extremely stress-reducing because you know it's okay to be yourself in your partner's presence—it's okay to be human. But this gift goes both ways. In other words, you not only want to be around someone who makes life seem easier and more fun, but you also want to be one of those people for your partner. If you can become less inclined to fight over silly little things, you will become far more desirable to your partner in every sense of the word.

Remember that, far from being stress-reducing, it's stress-producing and a real drag to be around someone who is always irritated at something you're doing and always picking a fight over some stupid thing. Why would you even want to be around someone who is always a second away from starting a fight? It's no fun, and it's incredibly stressful.

The solution is really quite simple; mostly it involves intention. The trick, it seems, is to begin to see irrelevant and unimportant things in their proper perspective. It's helpful to reflect on those things that are really important and to make a commitment to let go of almost everything else. Ask yourself the question, "Do I want my life to be about fighting over stupid things and demanding that everyone else, especially the people I love, be different?" By simply asking this question in such a direct and honest manner, the answer will become an obvious . . . no.

You'll begin to see that when you get annoyed and bothered enough to fight over stupid things, what you're really doing is defining yourself as a partner who is unable to stay focused on the gifts and strengths of your relationship. This can be a humbling, if not frightening, realization. Yet, it's an important insight. Because once you turn your judgments around in this manner and see how you are contributing to the problem, you can begin to shift away from this tendency—and instead learn to let the little things go and remain focused on what's right in your relationship. It's that simple.

We can't tell you how much more love you will experience and how much more fun you will have when you put this strategy into practice. From now on, when you catch yourself fighting over stupid little things, laugh at yourself and let it go. Make being happy more important than being stubborn. Soon this could be a habit that will change the course of your relationship forever.

Stop Wishing She (or He) Were Different

WITH KRISTINE CARLSON

There is no question that, philosophically, this is one of the most important strategies in this book. The connection between wishing our partner were different and our own level of dissatisfaction is powerful and significant. To make matters worse, this insidious habit is often invisible to ourselves, or at least very subtle.

When we love someone, it's tempting and perhaps almost inevitable to fall into the trap of yearning for a slightly "better" partner. This doesn't necessarily mean we actually want a different partner, only that we wish the partner we have was a little different from the way she actually is.

Whether we overtly acknowledge it or keep it to ourselves, almost everyone does this, however slightly. We might wish our partner were more like someone else, a better provider, more ambitious, gentler, a better listener, more passionate, better looking, less reactive, more helpful, or some combination of the above—but it's rare that it's not something.

The problem is, whenever there is a gap between what we have and what we want, we will feel dissatisfied or in some way frustrated. It's a hard-and-fast rule of life that applies to our relationships, just as it does to all other aspects of our lives. It's difficult, however, to make this connection because it seems, on the surface, that your lack of satisfaction is coming directly from your partner. The almost universal conclusion becomes, "If only my partner were different, or would shape up in some way, or change to meet my expectations, I would then be happy."

What most of us do in response to this seemingly logical conclusion is to yearn, fantasize, wish, hope for, or in some cases demand that our partner change. "By golly," we tell ourselves, "I'm not going to be happy until they do."

The result is that when our partner fails to change or to meet our expectations, we remain dissatisfied. We may even feel slighted or resentful because we are convinced that it is our partner who is preventing us from being happy. It's their fault. I could easily convince myself, "If only Kris would be more like I want her to be, I'd be happier," just as Kris could convince herself of the same thing about me. Either way, it's absolutely guaranteed that whichever of us continues to believe this to be the case will remain in some way dissatisfied. It's as predictable as the sun rising in the morning.

Unfortunately, even in those rare instances when our partner does change, any satisfaction we experience will be short-lived. When we attach our own happiness to the insistence that our partner change, it's only a matter of time before we need additional changes. I've met dozens of people—men and women—who desperately wanted their partner to become more helpful around the home. When their "dream" came true, either through conflict, compromise, or an honest effort by their partner, they quickly discovered that the changes weren't extensive enough. More changes would be better.

The trick is to see (and feel) the connection between the act of wishing that your partner were different from the way he or she actually is—and the corresponding and predictable feeling that something is missing, or not quite right. Once you see this dynamic connection between your own thoughts and the way you feel, you're in for an enormous surprise. In fact, your relationship will never be the same again.

As an experiment, take note of your dissatisfactions, the aspects of your partner that you wish were different. Now ask yourself the questions, "What would happen if I could stop wishing she needed to change to be complete in my eyes?" "What would happen if I decided to love her just the way she is?" Look for ways to love her as she is, right now.

When your attention shifts in this way, the changes in yourself will be noticeable and dramatic. Your demands will soften, and your dissatisfactions will begin to disappear. You'll become more accepting and forgiving, as well as substantially less judgmental. Your ability to communicate nondefensively will be enhanced, as will your ability to bring out the best in your partner. Finally, the love you feel will be more genuine and unconditional. The love you've been waiting to experience is within your own grasp. All you have to do is stop wishing she were different.

89

Jump-Start Your Relationship

WITH KRISTINE CARLSON

There's a widespread belief that the time to turn to experts is when your relationship is in trouble. After all, there's no question that a good psychologist, minister, priest, rabbi, social worker, marriage counselor, or other qualified professional can be enormously helpful during difficult times.

However, it's also the case that these as well as many other (including less traditional) professionals can be effectively used to jump-start your relationship, to push or encourage you toward growth, better communication, and increased love for one another.

Many relationships, even good ones, can become static or habitual. It's easy to begin taking each other for granted or to lose that wonderful spark that existed in times gone by. This doesn't mean there's anything wrong with your relationship; only that it could be even better. Often, a tiny shift in your thinking, a change of attitude, a dose of perspective, or a few new tips can make a world of difference.

I used to teach courses on happiness, which included, among other things, tips such as the ones you read about in my books. Often, couples would attend, not because there was anything wrong with their relationship, but because they wanted a little jump-start. One of my greatest compliments was when people would say, "That was just what we needed." What they learned was always very simple, just a little reminder of what it takes to be a happy person or a happy couple.

You can get the same kind of positive jolt by taking a class together on good communication skills or a workshop on becoming a more loving partner, or even sitting together for an hour-long lecture by one of your favorite authors or speakers. Many bookstores have free events where authors will speak for a while, followed by a book signing. There are audiotapes on relationship skills you can purchase, then create some quiet time to listen to together. If you prefer, you can read to each other out of a book that inspires you to become closer. Even something this simple can provide the jump start you're looking for. The act of doing one or more of these things is an acknowledgment to one another that your relationship is important, a statement that you want to continue to grow together.

We encourage you to start looking around for new ways to jump-start your relationship. It's a great way to spend time together and is almost always a great deal of fun.

90

Don't Sweat the Occasional Criticism

WITH KRISTINE CARLSON

Sometimes, when someone is criticized, you'd think by the reaction that we were in the midst of a national crisis! Many people get so upset when they are criticized—especially by their partner—that they not only get defensive and overreact, but they strike back, or even fall apart. If you look at criticism realistically, however, and with a bit of perspective, we think you'll agree that it's really not that big a deal.

The truth is, none of us is exempt from the rest of the human race. We're all going to get our fair share of criticism during our lifetime. And, if we're in a relationship, at least some of that criticism is going to come from our partner. It's inevitable because our partner spends a great deal of time with us. They see us at our best and at our worst. They know (and regularly witness) our weaknesses as well as our strengths. At times, we're around our partner when we are in really low moods and most susceptible to feeling criticized. If we're honest, we'll probably admit that this is the time we are most likely to criticize, as well.

In addition, we're around our partner during those times when they are in a low mood, when they are most likely to dish out some criticism. Let's face it. Our partner knows how to push our buttons and it's human nature to push them every once in a while when you're in a low mood. So, it's unrealistic—in fact, probably a little unfair—to expect that your partner won't, at times, criticize you. It's just part of being in a relationship.

When someone criticizes you, it doesn't mean they don't love you. Nor does it mean they don't respect or admire you. Criticism is just something that people do for a variety of reasons. Sometimes we criticize out of habit; other times it's because we're frustrated, confused, stressed-out, or insecure. Occasionally, we even criticize because we see a flaw that really does need to be fixed. In other words, not all criticism is unjustified. Often, it's actually constructive, even helpful.

The best way to deal with occasional criticism is to make allowances for it, and accept the fact that it is going to be directed at you from time to time. In a way, you have to expect it. It's similar to rain. You know it's going to come; you just don't know exactly when, and under what circumstances. And just like you wouldn't get mad at rain—you simply put up an umbrella and accept it—you don't need to be concerned about small amounts of criticism. All you need to do is allow it to be there—accept it, and let it go.

Often when you take this more philosophical stance and don't get so defensive when you're criticized, it seems to occur far less often and, when it does, it seems to fade much more quickly. For whatever reason, criticism feeds on defensiveness. When you react, it's as if the person doing the criticizing feels as though the criticism was justified and the need to criticize continues. On the other hand, when you let it go without ruffling your feathers too much, the urge and need to criticize fade into the distance.

Gale told me that her husband was usually a really nice guy but that he was sometimes critical of what he called her "lack of understanding of technology." Apparently, he loved to work with computers and couldn't understand why it was so difficult for her. I asked her how often his criticism was expressed and she said, "Probably three or four times a month." I asked her how she typically would deal with his comments. She said that she would usually become a little defensive and hurt. She also assured me that she had discussed the issue with her husband on many occasions, but that he just wouldn't stop.

I shared with her the essence of this strategy and she admitted that although she had never considered such a "passive" approach, she saw the logic and would certainly give it a try.

About a month later I received a really nice message from her saying that learning to deflect her husband's criticism was one of the easiest things she had ever done. She had decided to "reframe" his comments so that, each time he would begin his criticism, she would remind herself that what he really meant was that he cared about her and wanted her to benefit from the ease of technology. Rather than resisting his words, fighting back, and giving him something to hang on to, she would simply agree and say something like, "You're so right dear—I really should learn." Her lack of reaction was so unheated that he would drop it in a second. At some point he threw up his hands and said with a chuckle, "What's the use?"

Gale had turned her husband's criticism into a game. And she was learning to win! That's it, no big deal. There were no fancy techniques or heavy psychological issues to discuss or memorize—just a little perspective, a willingness to see the innocence in his criticism and to have a bit of a sense of humor. While there's no way to prove it, my guess is that had she continued with her defensive, take-it-really-seriously reaction, the criticism would still be there. As it turned out, it quickly disappeared.

Even if your partner's criticism is more serious or happens more often, this strategy should ease the pain. Without your reaction, there will be less energy to feed the criticism. Take it less seriously and it will begin to fade away.

Avoid Correcting Each Other

WITH KRISTINE CARLSON

We were in the lobby of a health club when a woman said to her husband, "See you later, honey. I've got to get home because I'd like to make you and the kids that casserole dish you love so much. It takes more than an hour and I want to have plenty of time." When I heard her say this, I thought to myself, "How thoughtful." My heart sank, however, when I heard her husband's response. Without even thinking about it, he fired back, "No it doesn't—it only takes about fifty minutes." Ouch.

A week or so later I was in a restaurant when I overheard a man telling a story to his wife and another couple at the table next to us. Obviously I wasn't paying much attention to the details, but he was talking for quite some time. All I heard was the last sentence, which he said with a satisfied chuckle. His punch line was, "We were just getting ready to leave when about ten people cut in front of us." It seemed like a good ending to a story and I found myself wishing I'd heard the whole thing. But before their friends had a chance to finish laughing, his wife blurted out, "There weren't ten people, John, there were only six."

Obviously these are somewhat obnoxious examples of the tendency many of us have to correct one another, particularly those we are closest to. Yet, we felt they were appropriate because they demonstrate how disrespectful and potentially damaging this habit can be to the quality of a relationship.

In both of these examples, and so many others, the "correction" was absolutely unnecessary. Other than being ignorant to the hurtful effects the correction has on the recipient, and the way it takes the joy out of sharing, the only possible motivation could be an attempt to be outright mean.

The woman in the health club was reaching out to her family. She was taking her valuable time and using it to express her love through her cooking. She was filled with enthusiasm as she proudly shared her plan with her husband. In return, he shot her down! There's no way to tell why he said what he did. My guess is he meant no harm and didn't even know he said it. But think about how it must have felt to her. What possible good did his comment make? Even if he was technically correct regarding the cooking time of the casserole, so what? How can being "right" be so much more important than protecting the feelings of someone you love? Rather than feeling appreciated, she probably felt minimized and deflated.

The same holds true with the wife who corrected her husband in front of their friends in the restaurant. Again, if you asked her, I doubt very much she would admit to ruining his story and his enjoyment and making him look a little foolish, on purpose. Instead, it was an innocent jab that took place because she hadn't taken the time to reflect on the destructive nature of correcting someone. Who cares how many people actually cut him off? What difference does it make?

Obviously, an isolated correction isn't going to make or break an otherwise nurturing relationship. We've all done it more than once. And keep in mind that if your partner corrects you every once in a while, you don't want to think of it as an emergency! It's not.

Remember, the goal is to stop sweating the small stuff. However, you have to wonder why a person would continue to share stories, dreams, plans, and adventures with someone who was in the habit of correcting them. After a while, if someone you loved kept up the corrections, you'd become cautious and guarded, perhaps even distant.

The lesson here is simple. No one appreciates being corrected. In fact, most people resent it. So, unless there's a really good reason or you're dealing with an extremely important issue, it's a good rule of thumb to keep your corrections to yourself. Your partner will be able to share with you freely and openly, which will help keep your relationship fresh and alive.

Don't Let Your Children Come Between You

WITH KRISTINE CARLSON

I believe that Kris and I have done a remarkable job in this category. We love our children more than words can say—we adore them, want the best for them, and, to a large degree, have dedicated our lives to them. They make our lives complete and there is no question that they are our top priority.

Yet, we love each other too. A ton! And we don't just say this—we mean it. We're great pals and best friends. We love to spend time together—to share, laugh, love one another, be silly, hang out, or just be quiet. We're partners.

We decided long ago that nothing—not even our children—would ever come between us. Furthermore, we realized, early on, that one of the most important messages we could give our children was to set an example as two parents who truly love and like each other; two people who prioritize one another *and* look forward to being together—even though we have a family to nurture and care for.

It appears to have worked really well. Both our children know how we feel about each other. They realize, on a deep level, that we have a mutual respect and admiration for each other, that we stick up for one another, agree on most fronts, and, most of all, that we love each other. There is no question in either of their minds. In fact, it's so clear to both of them that, when Saturday morning rolls around, one of them will usually say something like, "Where are you guys going tonight?" or "Who gets to babysit us tonight?" They assume we are going to go somewhere together because they know it's important to us—just as it's important for them to spend time with their best friends. To them, it would seem bizarre if we didn't.

Every set of parents is obviously different and will have different values and degrees of comfort where this issue is concerned. Our goal isn't to get other parents to prioritize their lives as we have. Yet, for us, we are positive that we are doing the right thing, not only for our relationship, but for our kids as well. Our guess is that their expectations regarding their boyfriends and future husbands will be fairly high. Our hope is that they will eventually seek partners who value not only their children (if they have them), but their relationships as well. We know many parents who, even years after having children, rarely go out alone—and a few who never have. It has always seemed to us that, even if you didn't like each other very much and if your only goal was to send a good message to your children about relationships—then you'd prioritize your relationship, at least once in a while. Otherwise, it would seem, they would grow up believing a "normal" relationship neither requires nor deserves any time or effort—the relationship would be seen as secondary, if not dispensable.

It's been said millions of times before—but worth repeating one more time: If you want a loving relationship, you must prioritize it and treat it as important. The truth is, you vote with your actions. You can say, "My marriage is really important," but your actions may be saying something entirely different. You may virtually never spend time alone with your spouse, or go out alone with her. Hardly the way you would behave if your goal was to appear loving. After all, you spend time with the kids and as a family, and you spend time at work, doing chores, shopping for "stuff," and in front of the television—so why not with your so-called loved one? Is that what you would hope for with your child—that he or she would grow up and never, ever spend time alone with their spouse, once they had children?

Finally, when you spend time together, even though you have children, you send a powerful message to one another that each of you matters, and so does your relationship. It's harder to sweat the small stuff with your partner when you both know that you are important to the other. So, however you do it, and to whatever degree, consider the importance of putting your relationship first. If you do, everyone wins.

93

Say the Words, "I'm Sorry"

KRISTINE CARLSON

I asked an acquaintance of mine a very direct question. It was, "How often does your husband say the words, 'I'm sorry?'" Her answer explains the necessity of including this strategy in this book. Her answer was, "You're kidding, right?"

It turns out that he never apologizes. She claimed that this is true, even when it's obvious that he made a mistake, caused her grief, or said something mean, insensitive, or condescending. This was a bit surprising because, on the surface, her husband seems like a really nice person.

I wondered if their situation was unique, so I began asking around. All in all, I must have talked to hundreds of people from all over the country. Much to my surprise, not all but most of the people I asked also reported that the words "I'm sorry" were a minimal, if not practically nonexistent part of their relationship. What's more, it turned out that even those who say the words "I'm sorry" often do so under their breath or mumbling, lacking a genuine sincerity.

I'm not sure why this is the case. It could be too much pride, a hardened ego, a lack of reflection, an inability to see oneself as part or all of a problem, or some combination of these things. Whatever the reason, I do know it's a mistake. Saying you're sorry, when appropriate, is an extremely healing and nurturing thing to do. It's seen by the recipient not as a sign of weakness, but of strength. It clears the air and opens the door to forgiveness and a fresh start. It brings trust, integrity, and humility into a relationship, three of the most beautiful qualities two people can share.

Luckily, we haven't had too many earth-shattering things to apologize to one another for. However, there have been times when Kris deserved a genuine apology and explanation for something I had done. Yet, even when the circumstances might have warranted a more insecure reaction, the apology proved to be the catalyst for enormous growth in our relationship, allowing us to talk about even painful things.

And we're not unique. It's extremely eye-opening to talk to couples who report that their partner does, in fact, use the words "I'm sorry" freely, when appropriate. They will tell you that, in many instances, the "mistake" that preceded the need for an apology was worth it, if for no other reason than the apology almost always brought them closer together as a couple. For example, Deborah had been overspending on her credit cards for years, which had created a multitude of financial problems. Her husband, Dan, had become quietly resentful. Each time they tried to discuss it, Deborah would either become defensive or, at best, she would claim she would "work on it."

I asked her if she was aware of the pain and fear she was causing Dan. She said that she was, but that she didn't know what to do about it. When I suggested she sit down with Dan and offer him a sincere, heartfelt apology, she became visibly uncomfortable. After a few moments, she said with a tear in her eye that she had been too ashamed and afraid to do so, but that she would try.

When I saw Dan again, he was happier than I had ever seen him. It turned out that he was more resentful of her lack of apology than he was of her spending habits. He said that her willingness to say she was sorry opened the door to deeper and less defensive communication, including their joint decision to visit a therapist.

Whether it's over major things or everyday minor things, saying the words "I'm sorry" will usually work to your advantage. It's one of those ever-so-important phrases to introduce to your relationship.

94

Treasure Each Other

WITH KRISTINE CARLSON

One of the most life-affirming, love-enriching messages you can send to your loved one is the message, "I treasure you." When someone knows they are treasured, they feel important and valued. This encourages them to treasure you back, to remain loyal and loving, and to feel as though your relationship is satisfying. When you get right down to it, letting someone know they are treasured is one of the greatest compliments you can give—and one of the best ways to say "I love you."

The best way to let someone know you treasure them is, you guessed it, to tell them. Be sure to let your partner know, frequently, what you like about them. Be specific. If you like their smile, their laugh, something they do, whatever, let them know. Don't make the mistake of assuming that your partner already knows what you like— they may not. You may not have told them for a long, long time.

One of the by-products of letting your partner know that you treasure them is that the positive aspects of your relationship are reinforced and strengthened. Your focus on your partner's positive traits, habits, and behavior keeps your attention on what's right with your relationship and what you enjoy about each other. It helps you dismiss the imperfections and keeps you from sweating the small stuff. In addition, when your partner is really clear about what you like

about them, they are far more inclined to repeat the attitudes and be-
haviors that you find so appealing. For example, if you tell your partner, "I love the fact that you almost always remember to say thank
you when I've gone out of my way to do something for you," he or
she will almost certainly continue to do so. Your positive feedback reinforces and solidifies an already positive characteristic. If, on the
other hand, you take this tendency for granted, and your partner
doesn't even know you appreciate it, there would seem to be a much
greater chance that it will fade away.

We have a close friend who is a psychologist specializing in,
among other things, marriage counseling. She tells us it's very common for people to know what their partner doesn't like about
them—but to have no idea of what they like or appreciate. No wonder they are in counseling! According to our friend, however, the
slightest acknowledgment, and more focus on the positive instead of
focusing exclusively on what could be or should be better, can turn a
relationship around. Her conclusions seem consistent with our own
observations.

One of the things that has always come naturally to the two of us
is our willingness to share what we like with one another. For example, I've always loved the way Kris can be silly—and she knows I like
it because I tell her. I also love how involved she is in the kids' lives,
how talented she is in creating beauty wherever she goes, how easily
she makes friends and makes people smile, and how incredibly forgiving she is. She, in turn, is quick to tell me she loves the way I'm
willing to help around the house and how good I am with our kids.
There are so many things we like about each other, and our willingness to share openly about our likes reinforces what is good in our
relationship. I'd guess that with few exceptions, Kris and I have told
each other at least one thing we like about each other every day since

we've met. Once, when we were having a rare conflict with one another, she said, "You know what, Richard? I really like the way you're willing to let go of things." You can imagine that we weren't mad at each other for very long.

Like most couples, we've been through many things in our time together—mostly good. However, one thing never changes: We really do treasure each other—and we hope you do too.

95

Have an Affair

I thought the title of this strategy would grab your attention and would be a great place to begin this section.

Okay, not that kind of affair!

The kind of affair I'm talking about is a love affair with life. If there's one thing I've noticed that seems to be lacking in many men, it's a passion for life. It seems that many of us have lost that sense of wonder and awe for the incredible gift of life itself. We've become lost in the multitude of responsibilities, ambitions, drive, and commitments. We've become very serious and heavyhearted. Many of us have lost our sense of humor and our perspective. We've lost our compassion, as well. Instead of marveling at it all, we take life for granted. We become stuck in the mundane and succumb to boredom. It's as if we're doing nothing more than putting in time and going through the motions.

Life is slowly passing us by. Without a genuine sense of enthusiasm, a zest for life and a lighthearted spirit, we take our problems and obstacles too seriously. We become uptight and a drag to be around. More than anything else, we start sweating the small stuff. Life starts to bother us instead of amusing us. People are seen as burdens instead of as gifts. Challenges are dreaded instead of seen as opportunities.

The solution to all of this is to have an affair with life. The idea is to reignite your passion for living, and to see the extraordinary in the ordinary. Remind yourself how precious and how short this adventure really is. I read a great book called *A Parenthesis in Eternity*. What a great way to think about the duration of your life—as a blip on a passing screen. We're here for a moment in time—and then we're gone. Why waste one second on self-pity, frustration, irritation, and all the rest? Our lives are so much more important than that.

It's shocking what happens to the quality of your life when you put it into this perspective. All of a sudden, the things that seemed so big seem small. And the things that seemed so small—and the things we postpone and take for granted—seem so big! We see that, for the most part, we usually prioritize in reverse order. But we can change all that in a moment. We can make a shift right now.

The things that we so often attach importance to are important, but it's a question of degree. Success, perfection, achievement, money, recognition—you can have them all, but they're not everything. In fact, without a passion and appreciation for life, they don't amount to much.

I was talking to a group of men about this subject. A few days later, I received a call from one of them that sums up the essence of this strategy. He said that while we were talking, he had thought that my "intentions" were good, but that I didn't really understand how serious and important his "role" was to everyone.

As fate would have it, while driving home that evening, his life changed in a single moment. He was nearly clipped by a huge truck on the freeway. He wasn't hurt, but it was a very close call. The near miss brought forth the insight that he hadn't spent virtually any time with any of his three children in several years, and that they were growing up very quickly. For the first time in years, tears came down his face as he realized that he was missing the point of life—as well as his chance to live it. When he arrived at home, he sat down with his family and told them that he was going to be making some changes in his life, beginning with appreciating his family. He had had a major change of heart.

Although this type of realization often has to do with family, it's not just about family. It's even larger than that. Recognizing the miracle of life—and having an affair with it—means that you begin to attach great value to the moments of everyday life. The people you live and work with—and, for that matter, go grocery shopping with—all take on far more importance. Nature appears more beautiful, life is more precious, conveniences are more appreciated. You become, not less effective, but less demanding on others and on yourself, because you better understand the relative importance and significance of the events around you. Things won't get to you so much, and you won't be sweating the small stuff—at least, not as often!

An affair with life is real, and it can happen to anyone at any time. All it takes is the commitment to reflect upon the miracle of life itself and to remember, each day, how lucky we are to be alive. Think about what it means to wake up in the morning and have another day to live. Someday, that won't be the case. In the meantime, live each day like it really matters—because it does.

One final note on this subject. Needless to say, an affair with life will never get you into any trouble with your wife or girlfriend. On the contrary, they will appreciate your change of heart as much as you do. So have fun.

96

Don't Let the "Turkeys" Get You Down

I believe this topic is so important that, a few years ago, I was going to write an entire book with this title. Eventually, I decided that instead of an entire book, I would wait for the perfect opportunity to include a few thoughts on the subject in an appropriate *Don't Sweat* book. That time is now.

As I reflect on my own life, talk to friends and acquaintances, and meet people all over the world, it's clear to me that one of the biggest challenges we face—of a relatively small nature—is to not let extremely difficult people (that is, turkeys) get us down.

I'm writing these words while sitting in the Burbank, California, airport. I just returned my rental car to a grumpy, impatient employee. There are hundreds of people around me, and most of them seem to be in an enormous hurry. A small percentage are smiling or laughing; the rest seem to be agitated and stressed.

As I sat down, a middle-aged man pushed a woman out of the way to secure his place in line before her. He then began to talk on his cell phone. His voice was loud and disruptive, and he was soon in an argument with the person he was speaking to. A woman in front of the same line was being extremely argumentative with the ticket agent. She seemed to think it was the ticket agent's fault that she couldn't catch an earlier flight, despite the fact that it was already full of prepaid passengers. As she stormed away, she threatened to sue the airline.

How many times in any given day do you meet a turkey? Some people do, in fact, seem to go out of their way to be difficult, demanding, conflict-oriented, hostile, or even obnoxious. How many seem to be such poor listeners that you wonder if you're being heard at all? I even heard of a man who seems to get some sort of thrill out of threatening people with frivolous lawsuits.

Because of our sometimes aggressive, competitive, or impatient nature, this subject seems particularly relevant to men. I believe that in order to live a truly joyful and fulfilling life, we must learn to respond to turkeys in a whole new way. After all, if we wait for the most difficult segment of society to change their ways, I'm afraid we're in for a very long wait.

Rather than feeling frustrated, disappointed, hopeless, and stressed-out simply because there are jerks in our world, we can instead learn to look the other way; to ignore them. The key, I believe, lies in stepping back and seeing how much attention a turkey tends to demand, and how that attention pulls you away from everything else that is going on—all the good, ethical stuff. It's actually quite fascinating.

You deal with dozens, maybe even hundreds of people each day. At least 95 percent of them are relatively polite, kind, and competent. Most people don't shove you, nor do they cut in front of you. Neither do most people interrupt you or flip you off. On the freeway, there are tens of thousands of drivers. There are a few aggressive bad apples, but a vast majority are just fine. In fact, I've asked many audiences the following question: If you have twenty things to do in a day and nineteen of them go well—which one do you talk about over dinner? Most people admit they'll talk about the one thing that went wrong. A similar question can be asked about people. If you deal with twenty people, and nineteen of them are normal, well-intended, relatively nice people, but one of them is a real jerk—which one is the subject of conversation?

Because the turkeys are by definition obnoxious, they will tend to steal your attention—they will pull you away from and encourage you to lose sight of everyone else, the 90 or even 95 percent of people who are nice, thoughtful, competent, and fair.

What seems to work like magic is to respond to turkeys as if they were the abnormality that they are. Don't give them the time of day—don't give them your valuable attention, your time, or even a second thought. By all means, don't give away your power to them. Turkeys thrive and feed on attention. So, when you see a turkey being himself, instead of feeding him with your attention, instead simply brush it off as one more jerk who is the exception, rather than the rule.

As simple as this sounds, it really works. Each time you see a turkey, rather than turning it into a big deal, thereby exacerbating the irritation you feel, it will become instead a reminder that most people aren't, in fact, turkeys. What a great way to turn a negative into a positive.

The result will be that, instead of being bummed out or angry when you see people being turkeys, you'll actually be reminded, instead, of how normal, kind, and together most people really are. The turkey will be the source of comparison—nothing more, nothing less.

Who would have thought that a turkey could actually be a good thing—a reminder that most people aren't like them? So, even when someone is obnoxious, even if it seems like it's on purpose, don't let it bug you—don't let the "turkeys" get you down!

97

Anticipate the Best

Three times this week, in three different cities, I heard a man say the words, "It's important to anticipate the worst." Each time, it was said in a conclusive manner, as if this was somehow a wise statement.

Benjamin Franklin once said, "I imagined some horrible things in my life—a few of which actually occurred." Most of us do the same thing. We worry, fret, get bothered, all worked up, and bent out of shape. The trouble is, a vast majority of the time, things work out anyway. So what's the point of spending so much time and energy imagining all these horrible things?

Consider, for a moment, the illogic of always assuming the worst. If what Franklin said is true, then most things will turn out fine. However, we tend to assume that they will not turn out fine. In fact, despite strong evidence to the contrary, we're going to assume that everything is going to go to hell in a handbasket. So, instead of easing through life—knowing that if we do our best and put the odds in our favor, all will be well most of the time—we're instead going to be stressed out and frantic for no legitimate reason. We're going to plan for the worst, spend our time and energy figuring out what to do if the walls come crumbling down, have intense conversations in our minds about all that could go wrong, and remain tense, agitated, and on guard. We're going to anticipate the worst.

Obviously, I'm not suggesting that that you don't think through the issues in your life, or plan ahead. Like you, I have contingency plans, I'm careful, and I carry life insurance. It's not about failing to plan, but instead it's about choosing to not spend your life immobilized and frightened about things that aren't likely to happen or those over which you have no control. One thing is certain: If you can eliminate (or greatly reduce) being worried about these two types of concerns, you're on to something important. You'll be far less stressed on a day-to-day basis, and you'll be a much happier person.

I hope you'll think about this strategy and give it a fair shot. You can certainly start with small issues, but I encourage you to start today. Instead of assuming that your conversation is going to be adversarial, assume it will result in a peaceful resolution. Instead of assuming someone is out to get you or take advantage of you, work on the assumption that most people are honest and that things will work out fine. You'll quickly discover that, most of the time, your new assumptions are going to be correct. I think you'll find that assuming the best is the best way to live.

98

Consider That "Needing a Vacation" May Not Be the Real Problem

I've heard the words "I need a vacation" so many times. And certainly there are times when we really do need one. We need to get away from our normal routine and do something totally different.

On the other hand, it's easy to convince ourselves that a simple vacation, a few days or a week away from our hectic routine, will ease the stress of our crazy lives—when the real problem is that our lives have become crazy. If that's the case, needing a vacation may not be the real problem—and taking one may not be the best solution.

Becoming overwhelmed doesn't happen overnight. Instead, it sneaks up on us. A few commitments and obligations turn into dozens. There is a funny but powerful saying regarding military defense spending: A billion here, a billion there; pretty soon it adds up to some big money. A similar perspective can be used in our own lives. Many of our commitments may not seem huge when seen in isolation; some in fact, may take only a few minutes to fulfill. However, combined, they can really add up.

There's an easy comparison on the subject of clutter. Have you ever stopped to think about how much stuff we collect? Much of it we don't even want. Mail, for example, pours into our homes to the tune of at least twenty pieces a day. Do you know that if you allowed twenty pieces of mail to come into your home each day for a month and didn't throw any of it away, at the end of the month you'd have almost 500 pieces of mail piled up? In a year, that number would soar to more than 5,000. And that's just mail.

It's the same with our lives. Many of us work forty, fifty, sixty, even seventy hours a week. Plus, we have important relationships, including children to love and care for. We have a home and perhaps a yard to take care of and projects to pursue. We may have pets. Many of us would like to squeeze in some exercise, maybe even a hobby or two. We have social responsibilities and are on various committees. We attend church or temple, and pursue other spiritual or religious disciplines, and in addition, we may volunteer our time.

If you keep adding things to your list—when you're already maxed out—at some point you'll go nuts; your circuits will burst. It's a wonder we do as well as we do.

I've found that reducing my commitment level has been far more beneficial than any vacation I've ever taken. Vacations, after all, last only a week or two. But reducing commitments and learning to say no is helpful 365 days a year.

The first step in finding a solution is identifying the problem. Take an honest look at your life and the number of activities you are involved with. If a vacation is appropriate, take it and have a great time. In addition, however, why not consider the possibility that needing a vacation may not be the real problem? An adjustment in lifestyle might be the real solution. This simple realization may help you bring the sanity back to your life. It did for me.

99

Let Others Be Right About the Little Things

I'm writing this strategy on a very crowded airplane. When we were boarding the flight, the man sitting next to me claimed that he had the aisle seat. He didn't. He was confused about the seat assignments, but he was determined to be right. I'm a frequent flyer and know the system quite well, and I prefer the aisle whenever possible, because I'm a very tall person.

At any rate, he was quite insistent, and I could see that he was going to make a fuss about it. Rather than turn it into a big deal, prove he was wrong in front of others, and have him mad at me for the next four-and-a-half hours, I simply smiled and said, "You're right, no problem."

Right about now you might be thinking one of two things. "Richard's a really nice guy," or "Boy, is Richard a pushover." And while I'd like to believe I'm a nice person, that really had very little to do with why I gave up my rightful seat (which, by the way, I had booked months in advance). I can also say, without much hesitation, ...t I'm really not much of a pushover either. When I feel the issue ... as tough as the next person.

... e up my seat had to do with the fact that in a v... ...s, it's simply not worth sweating it. I say th... ...good in this particular book, but becau...

I have found that a vast majority of the time, any satisfaction I receive in convincing myself and/or someone else that I'm right is far outweighed by the effort it takes and the negative feelings it brings to myself and the other person, as well as the conflict that is invariably created.

Think about what would probably have happened if my fellow passenger and I had gotten into a heated debate over the seat selection. (Believe me, I've seen this exact scenario played out on airplanes dozens of times, always with the same result.) We would have made a scene, and both of us would have been upset. Then, only one of us would have been able to get our way, leaving the other upset and angry. The person who secured the seat of his choice would have probably felt a tad guilty sitting there, knowing the other person was furious at him. There would have been tension. And for what? A preferred seat on a few hours' long flight.

It's a great analogy because it's symbolic of any of thousands of similar types of examples. Daily living lends itself to minor disputes or differences in opinion—happens all the time. Who got there first? Whose idea was it anyway? That's my parking spot—no, it's mine!

The less attached we can become to being right, the easier it is to stop sweating the small stuff. Does this mean it's never appropriate to fight for your seat or to prove yourself? No, of course not. Obviously, each circumstance is unique, and there's no hard and fast rule. The point, however, is that the emotional cost of being stubborn, defending and proving yourself, and of having to be right, far exceeds the benefits, in most cases.

100

Stop Broadcasting Your Thoughts

You've probably heard the expression "thinking out loud." It refers to the idea that, sometimes, it's helpful (or at least habitual) to be talking about our thoughts as we're having them. It's a way of sorting things out.

There's a fine line, however, between thinking out loud and what I like to call broadcasting your thoughts.

To the best of my knowledge, every one of us, at times, gets mad, frustrated, stressed, anxious, out-of-sorts, grumpy, tired, jealous, and all the rest of it. All of us have fearful, worrisome, angry, or pessimistic thoughts. That's certainly not news to any of us.

The question isn't whether we are going to have negative or self-defeating thoughts stream through our minds—we will. But rather, the question is what do we do with those thoughts when they are right there in the forefront of our thinking?

I've found that it's helpful to know that there are times that we can exacerbate and compound our feelings and problems by broadcasting the negative or insecure thoughts that happen to be in our mind. In other words, rather than seeing our thoughts as thoughts, and keeping them to ourselves, we announce them to others.

Suppose you're in the car with your wife and three kids. You're a bit tired and in a bad mood. At the moment, you're mad at one of your neighbors because she is planning to add on to her home, and you're anticipating a lot of extra noise from the construction.

In this case, there's nothing you can do about the situation. Her permits have been issued, and she's not doing anything immoral or illegal. Furthermore, you've added on to your own house over the years. It's not that big a deal.

But at this moment, you're just in a bad mood and your mind is looking for something to complain about. You're at a fork in the road. You can remind yourself that things always seem worse in a low mood and that you'll get over it. You can decide to keep your thoughts to yourself.

Or you can act on your impulse, which is to bring it up to your family and draw them in. You can broadcast your thoughts to your entire family.

But think about what happens if you broadcast these thoughts in front of your kids. They are going to think you're mad about something you can't do anything about. They probably don't know it's just a mood and that you may not even care about it the next day. In fact, they might imagine all sorts of problems between you and your neighbor. They might worry unnecessarily or even harbor ill feelings toward the neighbor. And while this is a pretty benign example, you have to ask yourself, To what end? What good does it do? And what does it accomplish? The truth is, there might not even be a real issue (other than in this moment) between you and your neighbor—but now your wife and kids think there is.

I'm not suggesting for a moment that there aren't hundreds of times when you will absolutely want to share what's going on in your mind with others. Perhaps most of the time, this will be the case. The trick is to be aware of the difference between sharing because you want to share and because it will be helpful or educational or whatever, versus simply blurting something out because you're having a frustrating series of thoughts.

This strategy can really come in handy and save you a lot of frustration. The next time you're having a thought attack of some kind and are tempted to share with someone else, take a moment to decide if doing so is really in your (and the other person's) best interest. If so, great. Go ahead and share. But if it's not, you might want to bite your tongue and wait for the thoughts to pass. In most cases, that's exactly what they will do!

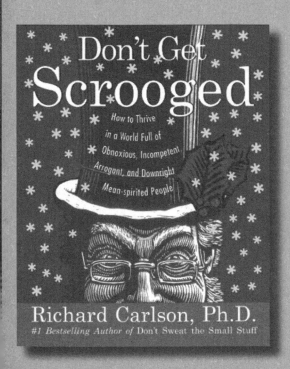